PRAISE FOR
EDUCATED BY DESIGN

"Rabbi Michael Cohen is passionate—passionate about teaching, about education, about creativity, and about sharing his passions with others. This book is his gift to you, filled with his lessons on how to design meaningful educational experiences that unleash students' creativity."

—Tina Seelig,
professor of the Practice, Stanford School of Engineering, author of *Creativity Rules*

"In *Educated by Design: Designing the Space to Experiment, Explore, and Extract Your Creative Potential*, Michael Cohen expertly blends anecdotal examples, practical advice, and big ideas about how teachers and students unlock their creative potential and share what they create with the world. A perfect book for those looking for a balanced dose of inspiration and a roadmap brimming with easy-to-try ideas."

—Adam Bellow,
cofounder, Breakout EDU

"Michael Cohen provides a bold vision for how educators can transform education by thinking like designers. This book will inspire you and challenge you as you innovate in your own practice."

—John Spencer,
professor and coauthor of *Empower* and *Launch*

"Teaching is a craft. Creativity helps it shine. All of us have creative capacities, and they can have a profound influence on student learning. In *Educated by Design*, Michael Cohen helps you find your creative teaching soul. If you've already found it, this book helps you refine it with practical ideas, activities for growth, and the inspiration to keep improving. Your students will notice the difference, and you'll notice the difference in your students' learning."

—Matt Miller,
author, speaker, and blogger, *Ditch That Textbook*, and 10+ year veteran teacher

"As someone who believes creativity is essential to all content areas, I find Cohen's book to be a breath of fresh air. It reminds us of the importance of creative freedom and creative confidence. Creativity is a mindset and something we can all achieve. Packed with the theoretical (why creativity matters) to the practical (a toolkit of ideas for incorporating creativity into your teaching), *Educated by Design* can benefit teachers of all grade levels and content areas. All classrooms today should have a deliberate focus on fostering creativity. Whether you are just getting started or a creativity pro, Cohen offers many ways for you to help all students develop their own creative mindset."

—Alice Keeler,
teacher, EdTech blogger

"I have seen Michael speak several times and have had the honour of talking with him. *Educated by Design* feels like a continuation of those conversations. You'll feel Michael's passion for learning and appreciate the clear connections he makes between the why of creativity and how to make it happen. It's an easy, valuable read that encourages readers to create their own solutions."

—George Couros,
innovative teaching, learning, and leading consultant
and author of *The Innovator's Mindset*

"Moving from a culture of consumption to one of creation and design is one of the most important steps educators can take to transform the learning experience, not just in their classrooms, but for themselves as professionals. In *Educated by Design*, The Tech Rabbi dispels many myths about creativity and design while providing practical ways to bring learning to life in your classroom. As Cohen shares, 'creativity is a mindset, not an art set,' so let this book help you design a recipe for disruption in your areas of influence!"

—Thomas C. Murray,
director of innovation, Future Ready Schools, Washington, D.C.

"Michael Cohen is someone who inspires me daily, and in his book, *Educated by Design*, he will inspire all educators. This is not just a book but a launchpad for creativity that is sure to put all readers in a creative mindset. Practical and inspirational, this vibrant thought-provoking text demystifies the creative process. This is a must-read for anyone looking to ignite a culture of creativity in their school."

—Laura Fleming,
educator and bestselling author of *Worlds of Making*
and *The Kickstart Guide to Making Great Makerspaces*

"Unfortunately, many of our students have been socialized out of their own creativity. Defeated by school environments that strongly emphasize compliance, they have sacrificed their creative natures on the altars of higher GPAs, better test scores, and discipline avoidance. This book shows us how to reignite the inner spark that resides in every one of our children and prepare them for a present and future world that rewards divergence, not convergence. It's an introduction to the key concepts of design thinking and creativity, complete with numerous concrete classroom examples of these principles in practice. It's also a call to action that will shift your mindset as an educator. Michael is an incredible designer of learning experiences for children. He can help you be one too."

—Dr. Scott McLeod,
associate professor of educational leadership and
founding director, CASTLE, University of Colorado Denver

"The Tech Rabbi always brings the truth! This book exemplifies his unique insights in education, creativity and design and is beyond the 'here are some tech tools' that other books sometimes offer. I love how Michael brings bold honesty to the world of education. He takes deep dives into the use of technology in schools, how failure can be a process for learning and different strategies for inspiring creativity. This book is a powerful tool for any educator or leader trying to reinvigorate and reimagine learning in school."

—Carl Hooker,
director of innovation and digital learning

"Michael Cohen is committed to empowering educators to develop a creative mindset. *Educated By Design* provides readers with the stories and experiences that have framed Cohen's perspective as both an educator and designer. Cohen provides questions to push your thinking on creativity in education and beyond."

—Monica Burns, Ed.D.,
founder of ClassTechTips.com, author of *Tasks Before Apps*

"Michael does an incredible job of disrupting and challenging mindsets with regards to creativity, design, and education. Creativity is not limited to the arts, and as he says, it is the spark, the catalyst, and the drive to view problems in new, unexpected ways. This book is a must-read for every educator looking to develop critical thinking, design thinking, and problem solving skills with students. What are you doing to design a recipe for disruption?"

—Brian Aspinall,
educator, author, coder, maker

EDUCATED by DESIGN

DESIGNING THE SPACE TO EXPERIMENT, EXPLORE, & EXTRACT YOUR CREATIVE POTENTIAL

MICHAEL COHEN, THE TECH RABBI

Published by Dave Burgess Consulting, Inc.
San Diego, CA
http://daveburgessconsulting.com

Cover Design by Genesis Kohler
Editing and Interior Design by My Writers' Connection

Library of Congress Control Number: 2018965584
Paperback ISBN: 978-1-949595-10-9
Ebook ISBN: 978-1-949595-11-6

First Printing: December 2018

TO MY PARENTS AND MY WIFE.

ANYTHING IS POSSIBLE
WHEN YOU HAVE SOMEONE
WHO NEVER STOPS
BELIEVING IN YOU.

CONTENTS

CONTENTS

FOREWORD BY DON WETTRICK

PRESIDENT OF STARTEDUP FOUNDATION, AUTHOR OF *PURE GENIUS*

For the past five years, I've attended several educational conferences and squirmed in my chair when the inevitable percentage of *uninvented* jobs quote crept up. You know the one: "By the time our elementary students enter the workforce 70 percent (or some similar percentage) will be doing jobs that have not been invented yet!"

This usually startles the audience, or makes them think about what jobs might be next. But what I want to do is stand up and scream, "Who do you think will *invent* those jobs? People who sit in rows, memorize things we already know, and await instruction? Or people who are allowed to invent, fail, reflect, and collaborate freely?"

I've played out this fantasy in my head. Every. Single. Conference. But I don't conjure up the courage, so I just shift nervously in my seat.

I've also seen, thankfully, a rise in awareness, an awakening, in thousands of educators concerned about that changing landscape of employment, and the urgency of adapting the educational experience. For me, it was with the 20-percent time, or "Genius Hour" movement coupled with the amplification of social media, that has gained momentum. More and more educators, parents, and students are showcasing amazing student work and using hashtags like #GeniusHour, #20Time, #PassionProjects, and #StuVoice.

Seven years ago, I launched a class called "Innovation and Open Source Learning" after introducing the 20-percent time model to my freshman English class. I had found that twenty minutes on a Friday just wasn't cutting it for those that wanted to *do*. I also found out that the twenty minutes were an uncomfortable challenge for my GPA-obsessed students. This made me clearly see the obvious divide in my class: those who wanted to learn something other than the standard curriculum, usually "C" students (or lower), and those that wanted to get an A.

After seven years, I've learned a lot about innovation, entrepreneurship, student motivation, and most sadly, the politics of curriculum. I wrote a book about the first two years of our class, *Pure Genius: Building a Culture of Innovation & Taking 20% Time to the Next Level*. I've become obsessed with getting more high schools interested in this type of class. I've been hosting pitch competitions, hack-a-thons, and even field trips to innovative work spaces. But there was one problem with my mission: I'm focused on an elective.

Then I met Michael Cohen (aka "The Tech Rabbi"). I knew from the day I met Michael that he has an understanding of creativity and the design process *for any class!* Michael has been talking to innovation gurus and teachers from all over the country. He takes what he learns and puts his newly enhanced toolkit into practice in the classroom. Yes, Michael is a teacher walking the talk!

Michael understands that Artificial Intelligence (AI), machine learning, infinite computing, and the Internet of Things (IOT) will render thousands of jobs obsolete in the next fifteen years. We've all seen the changes in our society creeping up on us. Self-checkout lanes, kiosks to order fast food, self-driving cars, and soon-to-be drone delivery. He also knows that because the experts agree that jobs that can be automated *will* be automated, educators must take a serious look at what will be in demand in the future. Michael Cohen and other top experts, are focusing on design and innovation because they understand that the students who are able to create scalable innovative designs will become the next generation's rock-star entrepreneurs.

Make no mistake, this book is not theory or inspirational based (although you will find it inspirational). We've all heard education experts stress the importance of "The Four Cs," but too often the critical thinking, communication, collaboration, and creativity don't reach beyond school boundaries. In contrast, this book is a guide to becoming more creative, letting empathy direct your design process, using rapid prototyping, and learning how to truly collaborate with a team.

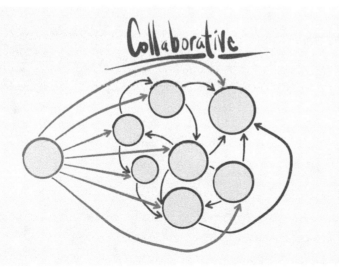

This book reads like a handbook to bring out the creativity in all students. You can go back to chapters, or even skip around because each chapter offers insights on important skills. Most valuable, however, is the peek you'll get into Michael's world as he transparently shares his journey. Please read this book with confidence, mark it up with notes, and tweet out your thoughts! The mission of instilling creative skills and a spirit of innovation in our students is essential and we, as educators and parents, must model journey!

THE BEAUTIFUL PARALLEL BETWEEN GOOD TEACHING AND GOOD DESIGN

I received an email. Not one of those emails letting you know that a website has updated its privacy policy. No, this was an email from a student, and I want to share it with you:

To: Michael Cohen Details

So I just thought of an idea for an invention that would be absolutely wonderful, but I immediately dismissed the thought because it's "not possible" and I "won't be able to do it."

Then I thought of you and how you don't dismiss creativity, so I wanted to let you know and see what you think.

Are you in school today?

Thank you for the inspiration,

Award-winning essays, honors and Advanced Placement courses, and a 4.0-plus GPA—this was the student who emailed me, and his words reminded me why I do what I do every day. This student, like so many others I have taught, lacked creative confidence, creative capacity, and most of all, belief. This student, one who on paper is a model student, has mastered the art of convergent thinking, an art of all things with singular correctness. The moment there is diversity, multiplicity, or an unknown, this student feels helpless. His lack of experience around divergent thinking makes him resistant to risk and fearful of failure.

As educators, we invest a massive amount of our energy into ensuring our students have the knowledge and skills to succeed in life. But how much time are we devoting to ensuring that our students can

BELIEF IN YOURSELF IN OTHERS

@thetechrabbi

successfully engage the abstract world? How are we preparing them to navigate a future that is both unscripted and unknown? How are we teaching them to trust their own intellects?

Innovation doesn't come from skill or knowledge alone; it comes from belief—belief in yourself, belief in others, and belief in something bigger than all of us. We want our students to believe that they have the ability to create something incredible, but for that to happen, they must experience the freedom of authentic learning. Our students must be allowed to take risks and be given the space to experiment, fail, and try again. Only then will they be able to leverage their skills and knowledge to take full advantage of those lightbulb moments.

> THOMAS EDISON WASN'T TRYING TO INVENT THE LIGHTBULB. HE WAS TRYING TO INVENT THE ABILITY FOR THE WORLD TO SEE IN THE DARK.

Thomas Edison wasn't trying to invent the lightbulb. He was trying to invent the ability for the world to see in the dark. What abilities are we helping nurture in our students? How are we helping them find their sweet spot? How can we help them believe that success isn't measured solely by money or skill? How can we teach them to value a project based on how much the world needs it or its support of the greater good? And what about us? How might we model this idea?

For some of us, education is a career, but for many of us, it's a calling. We need to make sure we have found our own sweet spot in the work we do. To do that, we must learn a thing or two from the world of design.

Education and Design

We are all educators. We are also all designers. We design new things every day! Our lessons, our classrooms, and our practice are all influenced by a design process. Design is about taking the obvious and expected and revealing the unconventional and potential from within. I believe all educators are designers!

I entered the field of education in 2009. I didn't consider myself an educator. I was a designer, creator, and a visual storyteller who happened to teach others about good design. In 2011, I was offered a job as a director of education technology, and at that point, I had to make the choice—designing or educating. I chose the latter. As I grew in the role, striving to create incredible programs and putting into practice a vision of meaningful and intentional uses of technology, I realized something powerful. I don't have to choose between design and education. Both are about creating opportunities for learning and leveraging creativity to solve interesting problems.

In 2016, I left my school to rediscover the sweet spot in the work I do. I had opportunities to travel around the world and engage incredible teachers, leaders, and students. It gave me a powerful new perspective and sense of gratitude. It also reignited my passion to contribute something great to education. In December 2017, I took a job as a director of innovation at YULA Boys High School to focus on developing programming around entrepreneurship and creative thinking. The goal of the program was to give students a time and place to work on refining their creative problem-solving process and abilities—to take a chance, mess things up, and then adapt and turn that mistake into something even better.

Revealing Creativity

I believe that creativity is a mindset, not an art set. Creativity is the ability to look at ourselves and the world around us and notice what isn't obvious to others and to author unconventional solutions to the problems we identify. We all are capable of this mindset because creativity comes from within. It's not something teachers give to students—it's something they reveal.

Too often in this life, creativity is purged by the fear or experience of being judged by others. Think about a time when you were in grade school and you created something you were proud of but someone else said it was bad. What did you do? How did that affect you? Those experiences are part of life. What we need to do is help our students develop creative confidence and creative capacity. That process starts by letting them explore.

Now, exploration isn't a free-for-all. Good explorers pack the right tools and resources, assemble the right team members, and most importantly, have the right mindset to keep moving forward in their journey.

What does that kind of exploration look like across K–12 education? Is it an after-school program? A lunch elective? Is it 20-percent time?

Wherever you start, you have to believe that you are helping your students on an important journey. In the chapters ahead, I will share some of my own students' journeys.

CREATIVITY IS A MINDSET, NOT AN ART SET.

King Solomon famously said, "There is nothing new under the sun." He was referring to the ingredients and their potential, not the next iPhone or the next unknown. A creative mindset requires us to shift our perspective with our tools and teams, but most importantly, our try. We have to try this.

Disclaimer: You will fail. Your students will fail. But when failure is part of the journey and not a destination, it can bring about significant growth. Remember, the greatest ascent happens only after the greatest descent.

Technology is not about the device; it's about what we can do with it. We must look at how technology can help our students become designers, authors, and creators of the awesome and the impossible.

We must show our students that learning is not confined to a classroom, and learning opportunities are everywhere. That means instilling in our students the belief that perfection should not prevent them from producing and publishing work that provides value for others.

We must show them the power of intentional design processes and to paraphrase Seth Godin, ship it and get their work out in the world.

I believe creativity is deeply rooted in kindness, goodness, strong moral character, and the desire to do good in the world.

Creativity is a social process.

So I ask you, how can we turn 20-percent time into 100-percent time?

Will you give your students the time and space to master a new skill?

Will you mentor them as they turn an idea to do good in the world into something actionable?

Will you give your students the confidence to share their gift and talent with the world because it brings value to others?

This is why I wrote this book. These students, the ones who have mastered the game of school but do not believe in themselves or have the confidence to take risks, will leave incredible ideas on the table for fear

WHEN FAILURE IS PART OF THE JOURNEY AND NOT A DESTINATION, IT CAN BRING ABOUT SIGNIFICANT GROWTH.

of failing, or even worse, of *being* a failure. This is why developing a creative mindset for a student is absolutely critical, and this is what our students need—to not just succeed in the world today but create a new reality for the world of tomorrow.

It might sound idealistic, but I see it as an opportunity to change what education looks like for our students. Beyond information and knowledge acquisition, beyond core literacy development, we can help our students develop creative confidence and the ability to experiment and accomplish incredible things in the world.

That's the difference between being educated, a convergent learning experience, and being educated by design, a divergent thinking one.

How to Read This Book

My desire when writing this book was to write it in a way that required you to read it straight through to the end. Such a practice would go against most of the book's content about how to design a meaningful, learner-centered experience.

I want you to live this book, not just read it. I use the derivative of the word *creative* 322 times in this book. That is because I want everyone who reads this book—and helps others because of it—to be able to look in the mirror and scream, "I AM CREATIVE!"

This book, without question, builds on itself, but each chapter also stands on its own, allowing readers to bolster specific skills or recap key concepts. The phases of each section focus on mindset, skillset, and implementation. In hopes of connecting implementation to mindset and skillset, I have given some general ideas about how each area can be successfully applied. Later in the book, you will find specific projects fully scoped out to see how each one of us can take our need mindset and skillset and apply those to our unique classroom situations and environment.

Note: The word *God* in Judaism is sacred, regardless of the language it is translated in. Throughout the text, you will see God spelled out as G-d.

CREATIVITY IS A SOCIAL PROCESS.

Creativity Is Deeply Personal

Creativity is about problem solving and it is also about personal branding. In today's world, it isn't enough for you to just invent something; you have to have a brand that reflects the value that you are trying to bring to the world. For me, I am not just an educator, designer, and struggling creative thinker (If you aren't struggling, you aren't thinking creatively.), but I am also a Chassidic Jew and a Rabbi at that. The Tech Rabbi brand is about merging together two very different fields to provide goodness and kindness in the world. At the International Society for Technology in Education (ISTE) conference in 2018, I had a Muslim woman approach me and ask me how I balanced technology and religious life. I shared with her the following excerpt from a book called *Hayom Yom* (Day By Day) an anthology of daily aphorisms. The excerpt reads as follows:

"THE JOB OF G-D IS TO TURN THE SPIRITUAL INTO PHYSICAL, AND IT IS THE JOB OF EVERY PERSON TO TURN THE PHYSICAL INTO SOMETHING SPIRITUAL."

This means that the purpose of all the tools in the world, including all technology, is to provide positive, good, and constructive value to us and those around us. As a Rabbi, I am committed to guiding those around me in succeeding in this mission. As an educator, I am committed to supporting students and teachers around me to independently succeed in this mission. The mission, simply put, is to leverage the skills and creative thinking of today to make the world a better place than it was yesterday.

I launched the Educated by Design project in 2017 with the realization of how much my experience as a designer influenced my teaching practice. That doesn't mean educators need to quit their jobs and become designers and creative directors, but I believe my experiences can be a valuable lens to look through as we imagine ways to better engage and support students. I will say that I believe all teacher programs should require two to three exploratory courses required to help pre-service teachers develop self-awareness and tap into their passion. These two ingredients are really the flour and sugar of the Educated by Design recipe. Regardless, *everyone* is able to nurture and master these two areas to bolster their creative process and abilities.

Creativity is so much more than the talents you possess. It's the way you think and see the world around you. Designers tackle problems head-on. Their livelihood relies on helping solve problems that others are not able to. Sound familiar? It should because outside of creative professionals, educators are one of the few professionals tasked with converting abstract potential into something tangible and measurable. Design has a similar launch point. You have a client who has an Idea, maybe even a vision, and you are the one charged with concretizing that vision into something clear, concise, and continuous. For me as a designer, educator, and someone who strives to have a growth mindset, I see so many powerful correlations between the process of design, teaching, and learning.

I once had a client hire me to create a corporate identity for their company. This meant not just designing one of the products for them like a business card, letterhead, or signage, but all of the components had to connect together to communicate a message that represented the best in quality, success, and good character of the company. This process was long and arduous with many setbacks and failures, which I, of course, as the designer had to shoulder. The client simply didn't get that I WAS THE EXPERT and that my advice was what was needed to succeed. My ears were closed, and as long as my guidance wasn't final, the project was stalled, and I wasn't budging. It was at that moment that I realized something. It was a powerful message

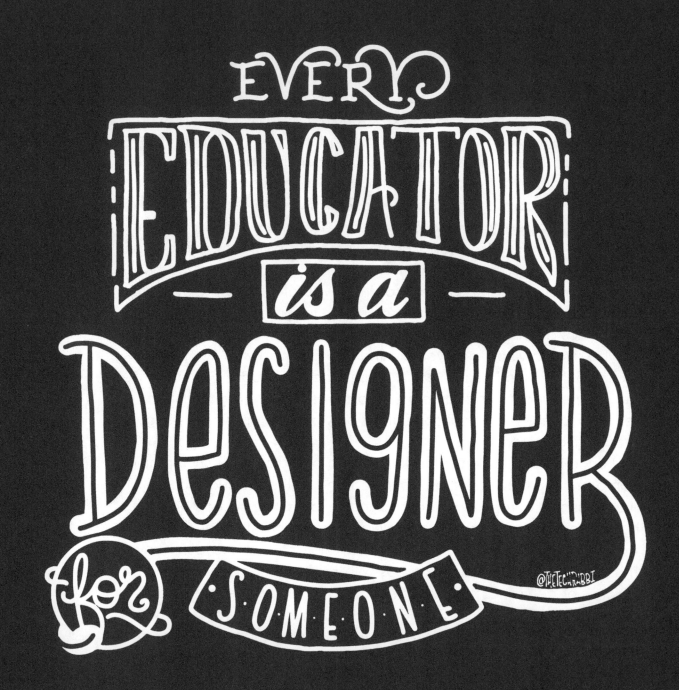

that mixed in customer service, quality assurance, and a solid dose of humility. But how could I let the customer be right? How could I sacrifice what I knew to be good design principles to make the customer happy and get their way? What would that make me? A fraud? A novice? A second-rate designer? This micro view missed out on some macro opportunity. You see, good design is about people. Dieter Rams once said that "you cannot understand good design if you don't understand people," because each one relies on the other to establish value and meaning. In the end, I became committed to putting the client and their needs first. This would ensure that I would design the best products for them and not for myself.

Does this story sound familiar? While you might not consider yourself a designer, you in fact are, and I plan to show you through the following story.

I once had a student that I taught in an advanced writing course. My job was to teach them foundational literacies, such as reading, writing, and verbal communication, as well as how all of those components connect to communicate a message that represented the best in quality, success, and good character of the student. This process was long and arduous with many setbacks and failures, which I, of course, as the teacher had to shoulder. The student simply didn't get that I WAS THE EXPERT, and that my advice was what was needed to succeed. My ears were closed, and as long as my guidance wasn't final, the learning was stalled, and I wasn't budging. It was at that moment that I realized something. It was a powerful message that mixed in customer service, quality assurance, and a solid dose of humility. But how could I let the student be right? How could I sacrifice what I knew to be good teaching principles to make the student happy and get their way? What would that make me? A fraud? A novice? A second-rate teacher? This micro view missed out on some macro opportunity. You see, good teaching is about people. Dieter Rams once said (not quite) that "you cannot understand good teaching if you don't understand people," because each one relies on the other to establish value and meaning. In the end, I became committed to putting the student and their needs first. This would ensure that I would support the best learning for them and not for myself.

I hope you can appreciate that moment. Very few professions overlap in such an interesting way as teaching and design. I tried it with marketing, nonprofit management, and sales, all three areas in which I have a professional background. There is something genuine about good design, and I see the very same thing in good teaching.

Whether it is in the process of design, the experience of design for others, or the moment where you become the gap between an idea and its implementation, I believe that educators can gain a great deal from incorporating some aspect of design into their ways of thinking and classroom practices.

The approach above is nothing new in education. You would be hard-pressed to find a school that would not promote itself as student-first or student-centered. In practice there are so many factors that influence, impact, and impede our ability to support our students at that level. Does that mean that design is the magical recipe for student success? It might not work for every teacher and every student in every classroom? No. Still, I believe that most of my success as an educator and an administrator supporting educators is due to my understanding of good design.

In June of 2017, I was fortunate to be one of the keynote speakers for the ISTE conference. It was a definitive moment for me. While speaking to a room that held 10,000 people felt like an incredible validation of years of hard work as an educator, speaker, and entrepreneur, I was still scared to stand on that stage. I have spoken to crowds in the thousands,

and I love speaking. I love storytelling and being able to craft a message that takes an audience on a journey. I leverage my gift of art to creative slides that help amplify that journey, many of them contained in this book, but I was scared. I wasn't scared of the crowd size. I wasn't scared I would fumble a line or miss an important idea. I was scared that I would stand on that stage and share my message of creative courage and capacity, and the incredible educators in the audience would think the five most horrible words possible:

He's right! But not me.

As I finished the talk and soaked up for a moment the applause and cheers, I went backstage and slumped down on the couch. I opened Twitter and saw the responses. I saw educators in the thousands take photos of my slides and build on the message. I saw them express gratitude, thanks, excitement, and confidence, but most importantly, I saw that they believed. They believed that they could create and that their students could express their creativity if just given the chance. It took hours to run through all the messages, and as I tried to engage with each and every one, I, too, believed that the audience, these amazing educators, were not just thinking but saying:

"He's right! I can do this!"

I didn't know where to put this story in the book. It's here because we as educators, mentors, and advisors have to understand that we are gifted, we are talented, we are skilled, but that is what G-d gave us. At the end of the day, I am a Rabbi, so for me, it's G-d Almighty. Each one of us has to come to terms with our own higher power, something that is bigger than ourselves. When you have that, you have something to fall back on as you continue to embark on a selfless calling of being a teacher, a trainer, and a torch that will help guide those precious souls in your classroom. Humility can only exist when you're doing something great and providing value for others. It's how you're changed after realizing your greatness and knowing how to value those that you engage with over why they look to you.

I won't lie; the 300 or so selfies I took after that keynote speech were a mixture of discomfort and awesomeness. What it showed me was when you provide value for others, when you give of yourself to see others succeed, you will achieve greatness, but you have to always remember:

Never stop creating.

Let's collaborate together as we all embark on this creative journey. Create, capture, and curate your experiences on Twitter and Instagram by using the hashtag #EducatedByDesign and tagging me @TheTechRabbi.

FIND THE LINKS MENTIONED IN THIS BOOK, ALONG WITH EVEN MORE RESOURCES, TIPS, AND INSPIRATION AT THETECHRABBI.COM/EBDTHEBOOK

CHAPTER 1

CREATIVITY IS A MINDSET, NOT A TALENT

**Our mission on earth is to recognize
the void—inside and outside of us—and fill it.**
—The Lubavitcher Rebbe

**Once in a while you get shown the light
in the strangest of places if you look at it right.**
—Grateful Dead

What is creativity?

When I ask people that question, their answers tend to associate the creative process with a talent, usually something artistic or musical. But true creativity isn't limited to the arts. Creativity can fuel countless talents and skills and gifts because it comes from within an individual. It's the spark, the catalyst, the drive to view a problem—or perhaps even life itself—in a new and unexpected way. Creativity is found in the way talented people use their talents. It's found in their thinking, wondering, exploring, and their embrace of the unknown. It's the mindset that allows their talents to thrive.

What about those folks who aren't artistic or musical? What about those of us who can't dance or sing or draw or sculpt or craft or act? What does creativity look like for us? I believe it must take a different form—one not focused on creating something from nothing but on creating something into something more. Today, creativity demands something more from our minds, our souls, and how we look at the world around us.

Growing up in school, I was told that creativity is not a job. Today I make it my job to be creative and help others develop the same thinking and strategy to achieve above and beyond their goals and expectations.

I have learned that not everything you need to know in life is learned in school, and that it is never too late to learn something or become something. If Sidney Frank can create a business around Grey Goose Vodka in his seventies, none of us have an excuse. Sidney, who was already a successful businessman, could have continued with the status quo. What he showed the world is that it is never too late to create something new and great, and creativity might be lying in plain sight, and just eight years after creating the new Vodka, he sold it to Bacardi for $2 billion.

That fear to leap is what keeps so many of us stuck in the status quo and fearful of the potential of failure. In 2016, I attended the SXSWEdu

IN SCHOOL I WAS TOLD CREATIVITY IS NOT A JOB. TODAY I MAKE IT MY JOB TO BE CREATIVE.

conference. With a messenger bag slung around my shoulder and the tired look of travel on my face, I checked into my room at a hotel in downtown Austin. My concierge smiled and asked me what brought me to Austin, and I told him I was speaking at the conference about how to develop a creative mindset to better identify problems and develop solutions for challenges we face. He smirked, like so many before him, as he said something like, "I wish I was more creative" or "I'm not creative." Either way, something had convinced that guy he wasn't creative even as he was getting a master's degree in film production while working nights as a concierge at a posh Austin hotel. What is it? Is it our schooling? Could twelve years of solving linear problems explain our tendency to view life's challenges through the lens of a standardized exam? Perhaps. The good news is that while our current education system might not be designed for creative thinking, it is still possible to develop a creative mindset.

Somewhere around age six, the current education model begins to purge students of creativity, curiosity, and wonder. The purge is so extreme that pedagogical models such as inquiry-based learning can not only exist but also be considered revolutionary.

Has any revolutionary invention, process, or approach been achieved without inquiry?

Step back for a moment and think about that. Our education system, a system meant to prepare young people for a future of success, is designed in a way that a model of learning based around posing questions, problems, and scenarios and seeking to solve can be considered innovative. Now don't get me wrong; I think that inquiry-based learning is an amazing concept, but its birth stems from a system of standardized learning that is linear and multiple choice. So how do we re-infuse education with that creativity and curiosity that is purged so soon? How do we incorporate it into our teacher practice, our classroom

I'm not creative...

learning, and into the culture of our schools and institutions? The first step is to shatter the myth that creativity is a talent and the stereotype that equates creativity to being artistic, musical, or skilled in some other expressive process.

When we finally understand that creativity is a way of thinking that blends our imagination with the world around us, true innovation can exist, and it doesn't need to be at the level where lightbulbs are invented. Innovation for a first grader might not be groundbreaking for a ninth grader, but it is important to remember that value is subjective when analyzing the creative process for different age groups. Creativity is a mindset, not an art set.

CREATIVITY ISN'T SOMETHING YOU GET; IT'S SOMETHING YOU REVEAL.

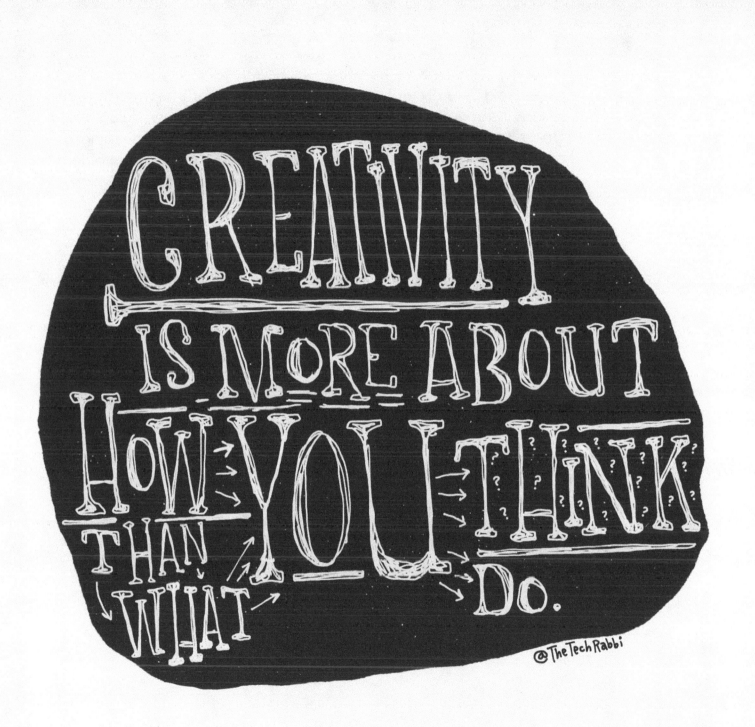

As I said before, creativity isn't something you get; it's something you reveal. It's about divergent thinking, a term coined by psychologist J.P. Guilford to describe the process of creating ideas by generating as many solutions as possible. The divergent-thinking approach to problem solving stands in stark contrast to today's educational system, which is built on convergent thinking, a method of discovering a singular "correct" answer.

I believe both divergent and convergent thinking have a role in life, but innovative practice and process are more likely to thrive when we create new ideas and solutions. We often associate creativity with originality. While a factor, it is not always required, and many times, it is the improvement of something that already exists that results in an innovation.

HOW DEVELOPED IS YOUR CREATIVE THINKING?

In the toolkit in the back of the book, you'll find a link to a sample Torrance Test of Creative Thinking (TTCT). Testing yourself and giving your students an opportunity to take it can open up a window into how developed our creative thinking is. Similar to assessing yourself during marathon training, it helps to know what you are capable of doing now as well as the growth you hope to achieve.

CREATIVITY
is a [MINDSET]
not an [ART SET]
- THE TECH RABBI -

FUNCTIONAL FIXEDNESS IS ONE OF THE GREATEST OBSTACLES OF CREATIVITY.
– THE TECH RABBI

The Obstacle of Functional Fixedness

If we're open to shifting our thinking, what is the next step? I believe it's found in the words of Steve Jobs, who shared in the 1994 interview that "Creativity is connecting things." Our ability to connect people, places, and ideas is rooted in how we view the world, and in turn, that worldview determines how easily we are able to overcome one of the greatest obstacles to creativity—functional fixedness.

What is functional fixedness? It is a cognitive bias that results in an inability to use a known object in a new way. In plain English, this means that a box is used to hold one thing, a shoelace is for tying shoes, and a toothpick is useless if you have nothing stuck in your teeth. The research around functional fixedness began to take form in the mid-1940s, when gestalt psychologist Karl Duncker started to research the method in which we solve problems with limited yet familiar resources. His most famous activity, the "Candle Problem," is one that might look familiar to you. I saw it first in Daniel Pink's book *Drive*, yet for some reason, I couldn't share that I had seen it before. Sure enough, I dusted off my educational psychology textbook from grad school, and there it was in chapter 8!

What is it about the problem that is so powerful? In workshops, I have seen some people solve it in less than five minutes while others struggle well past half an hour to reach a solution. The problem helps us understand the mental barriers preventing us from looking for novel and unconventional solutions to the challenges we face. One way to overcome this functional fixedness is to engage in diverse experiences and interact with individuals who have diverse backgrounds.

Before becoming a professional educator (I have always considered myself a teacher), I was by trade a designer, artist, strategic marketer (fancily referred to as a storyteller these days), and a businessman. I believe all of those experiences shaped my thinking and my approach to education. Don't get me wrong—I am not telling teachers to get a

second job, nor am I questioning the validity of teacher programs, credentials, and advanced degrees. (I have a master's in education, after all.) I am, however, challenging everyone reading this book to diversify their resources and connections when looking to hone their educational craft. The true first step of developing a creative mindset is to identify and learn from creative people in a wide variety of industries.

LEARN FROM CREATIVE PEOPLE

Here is my shortlist of those who have influenced me, inspired me to shift my thinking, and helped me succeed. They are talented, creative, resilient, and most importantly, patient—a characteristic that easily deserves its own book. These individuals are leaders in core areas that I feel are critical for learning what a creative mindset looks like:

ENTREPRENEURS

Gary Vaynerchuk is a serial entrepreneur, media marketing master, author, and social media extraordinaire. He also curses like a sailor, which makes it slightly awkward for a rabbi to endorse him. At the end of the day, his message that anyone can make it if they are patient, stick with it, and put in the work is tried and true for me.

- Twitter: https://twitter.com/garyvee
- Site: http://www.garyvee.com
- Content: https://youtu.be/1ClbiB7_YYg

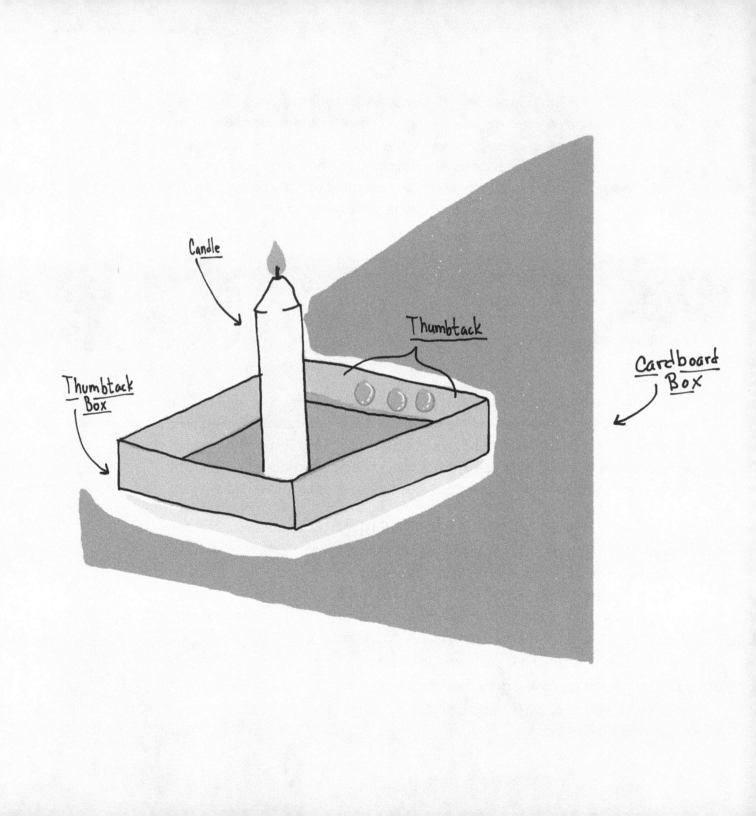

Seth Godin is an entrepreneur, author, and speaker. He has published eighteen bestselling books, many of which have significantly impacted me and my work, including *Linchpin* and *What To Do When It's Your Turn (and it's always your turn)*. His insights into how we communicate ideas, build confidence around the value we can provide others, and the need to just "Ship It" and get thing out into the world are not just inspiring, but actionable directives to helping prepare our students for tomorrow.

- Twitter: https://twitter.com/ThisIsSethsBlog
- Site: https://www.sethgodin.com
- Content: https://youtu.be/xBIVIM435Zg

DESIGNERS

John Maeda is a designer, technologist, and creative driver in education and business. As a former president of Rhode Island School of Design (RISD), professor at the MIT Media Lab, and consultant to startups, he has mastered the way in which design and creative thinking can influence business to succeed.

- Twitter: https://twitter.com/johnmaeda
- Site: https://www.maedastudio.com
- Content: https://www.designintech.report

David Kelly is an entrepreneur, designer, engineer, and teacher. He is a founder of the design firm IDEO and a professor at Stanford University. His work has had a huge impact on me since I first saw his team at IDEO featured on an episode of *Nightline* in 2012. I have come to think of him as a distant mentor as my own design thinking continues to grow and evolve.

- Twitter: https://twitter.com/kelleybros
- Site: https://www.creativeconfidence.com
- Content: https://youtu.be/M66ZU2PCIcM

ENGINEERS

Tina Seelig is the head of Stanford University's Technology Ventures Program and an author of many titles, including *What I Wish I Knew When I Was 20*. Her book changed my life forever, and I looked to her many times while writing this book.

- Twitter: https://twitter.com/tseelig
- Site: http://www.tinaseelig.com
- Content: https://youtu.be/gyM6rx69iqg

INVENTORS

Elon Musk is possibly one of the greatest inventors and engineers in history. He has innovated more industries in the past ten years than some could do in that many lifetimes. Beyond creating the first reusable rocket and the fastest, most epic, electric car, he is a huge philanthropist who takes action to help communities in need. He is a huge inspiration to me and the work I do.

- Twitter: https://twitter.com/elonmusk
- Content: https://youtu.be/QygpaJJclm4

CREATIVE LEADERS

Sir Ken Robinson is an author and international speaker on education in the arts. His 2006 TED Talk on how schools kill creativity has been a major influence on me, as an educator, and the contents of this book.

- Twitter: https://twitter.com/SirKenRobinson
- Site: http://www.SirKenRobinson.com
- Content: http://bit.ly/Robinson-ChangingEducation

Now that we're open to shifting our thinking and having resources to inspire us, we must overcome the second greatest obstacle to creativity, and that's failure. The odds are high that whatever we're attempting is not going to work the first time, or the second time, or the tenth. We must be patient, reflective, and go all in on a long-term basis and not let the short-term tell us our efforts aren't worth it or that the world is fine just the way it is. In today's system of education, when something does not work perfectly or perform well the first time out, we chalk it up to failure, assign it the appropriate letter grade, and move on. To an educator with a creative mindset, a setback is not only an acceptable and foreseen risk but a springboard to success down the road. To an educator with a creative mindset, failure doesn't mean giving up on a vision. It means slowing down, adjusting, looking at the problem from a different angle, or even teaming up with new people to brainstorm. Mostly, it's having the ability to embrace the unknown and seek out others—students, colleagues, mentors, or even competitors—to journey with you.

Creativity Beyond Talents

When asked what creativity is, we inevitably associate it with action—talents such as art, music, and cooking rather than a mindset that can actualize those talents. That tendency is not our fault. Look up creativity in the dictionary, and you will find a definition focused on original ideas and artistic work. I see creativity differently. I believe that creativity is, first and foremost, a mindset, a thought process, and a method of analyzing the world around us. It's an experience, and it goes beyond making something from nothing and, instead, turning something into something more.

In Old Testament scripture (Ecclesiastes 1:9), King Solomon says, "There is nothing new under the sun." This statement is powerful because it proposes that newness isn't found in nothingness but rather in the mixing of elements and experiences that occur throughout our lives. He was referring to invention and innovation. I have carried it with me through my journey as an artist, designer, and professional educator, and the idea it conveys is something I live by daily. I have always had a passion for teaching and helping others. As I look to connect Biblical wisdom to modern innovative ideas, I find that many of Steve Jobs' insights reinforce and expand upon King Solomon's words. Jobs' entire unconventional life was marked by innovation. He did not allow traditions, trends, or popular expectations to dictate how he changed the world. For Jobs, creativity was about forging connections and having diverse experiences. In his 2005 "Stanford Commencement address," he shared a story of how, only after he dropped out of college, he was able to take a course on calligraphy that interested him but, due to a series of prerequisites, he was prevented from taking it when he was enrolled. While I am not proposing our youth drop out of college, by any means, it is important to note that, while school strives to give our students a diverse and broad set of experiences, most learning that occurs in K–12 occurs through predefined and standardized experiences with a singular outcome or expectation. Truly, creativity thinking occurs through diverse experiences that challenge you to find ways to solve problems that don't exist in a linear fashion.

While models of innovative problem solving like design thinking are great at tackling large and complex problems, it is this diverse experience that will aid you in coming up with novel solutions to even the simplest challenges in everyday life. Developing a creative mindset and thinking like a designer requires the ability to broaden one's understanding. For educators, that might mean casting a wider net than previously expected. An effective way to broaden thinking and diversify experience is to connect with colleagues from other areas of your school or organization or even in other fields.

I once ran a design-thinking workshop at a major national university. The workshop attendees comprised an amazingly diverse group of professors spanning the schools of business, health, music, sciences,

and engineering. These professors had never met one another, and with a student population of more than 30,000, that wasn't surprising. That workshop was about much more than teaching faculty members to understand and use the design thinking method. Those educators, with their diverse backgrounds and experiences, were able to solve challenges in ways that would have been impossible otherwise. Through empathy and ideation, the participants were able to better understand and begin to address some of the challenges students faced in college. While some groups chose to find ways to make learning more real world, others sought to empower students to strive beyond "getting an A" by engaging in meaningful work. While observing them work, I thought about what would be happening if the groups were made up of professors in similar disciplines. Would they be more comfortable? Yes. Would they come up with ideas more rapidly? Most likely. Would the lack of diverse experiences and expertise limit how creative their ideation was? It is hard to tell, but I would venture to say yes as I watched professors of music, business, and biology blend their unique backgrounds and approaches in learning to solve the problem of student engagement in novel and creative ways.

These kinds of social interactions and engagements are critical to developing a creative mindset. Remember, creativity is about thinking broadly, and that is achieved by looking beyond ourselves and our closest peers and colleagues for inspiration. When I was a director of education and information technology, one of my roles was solving technical issues that no one on my team was able to resolve. On one occasion, I sat in the empty gymnasium, trying to resolve the issue with our presentation equipment at a K-8 school where I worked. The MacBook was able to project video through the HDMI cable, but no matter what I did, I was unable to get the audio to do the same. Unable to resolve the issue, I decided to search YouTube to see if someone had already

A CREATIVE MINDSET IS DEVELOPED

solved the problem and create a step-by-step tutorial to fix it. What I didn't realize was that I had the projector on, and all of my activity was being projected on the big screen as an eighth grader watched me from the door. As I finished up and turned to leave, I was surprised to see her standing there. She said, "Rabbi Cohen, I didn't realize you needed YouTube to fix things. I thought you knew everything about technology." That moment taught me something powerful. First, always check to see if your projector is on. Second, students are (or, at least we hope they are) just as interested in discovering how we as educators learn as they are in learning the content themselves. The outcome from the encounter led me to design an elective course that included, among other things, a unit on how to effectively search the internet for solutions to our problems. Once again, it isn't about coming up with new ideas yourself; it's about using what you have in new ways.

A creative mindset is developed partially by broadening our experiences and our thinking by engaging with individuals outside of our field, especially if we are already in the midst of a career with no plans to diversify our own work experiences. Remember, creative thinking is what leads to creative processing, not the other way around. Think about today's advancements in technology and what we are able to do. Think about the processes and activities that have been simplified to the point that a kindergartener is able to complete what was once a high school activity. I'm talking about video production, a skill that once required multiple devices and hours of training. Now it can be used in elementary school classrooms—with ease and flair—to teach children about butterflies. Today first graders across the country regularly script, film, edit, and produce their own educational films. That is pretty insane if you think about it! Even more, look at the advancements in educational resources that give you the ability to acquire a skill in just about anything by watching a YouTube video, enrolling in a Massive Open Online Course (MOOC), or taking an online course from a top university.

Technology has transformed our world and continues to offer us myriad ways to explore creativity. A robot can be programmed to paint the *Mona Lisa*, play Mozart on the piano, all while cooking cuisine inspired by Morimoto. But if the creative process is void of thoughtfulness, passion, and inspiration, it's nothing more than mere imitation. True creativity stems from the desire to impact people and change the world around them. This can occur in a classroom or an office, and it can spread from your local community and beyond. While creation for the sake of creation is possible, it is the social connection that drives creativity to new heights.

Applying Creative Thinking

Creativity, by nature, is difficult. It requires hard work, practice, and commitment. The challenge is that creativity is abstract at best and ambiguous at worst. Where does creativity start? Where does it finish? How do you proceed when you resolve to apply creative thinking to a specific problem or project or initiative? When most people embark on a creative journey, they're excited to tests out their ideas. One model that truly inspires me is released annually by the Gartner Group. Gartner's Hype Cycle (such an awesome name) is a model in which the

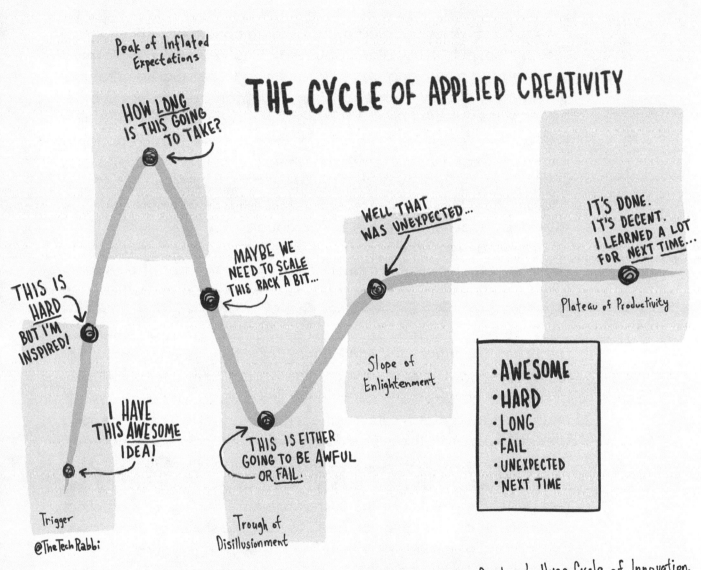

company projects the current pace in which emerging and maturing technologies will be adopted by mainstream consumers. After years of seeing them publish updated cycles, watching virtual and augmented reality trudge along, and smart dust seeming to be stuck in perpetual emergence, I began to see how this cycle can be applied to other topics, including the creative process. The reason for this is that I find that applying creativity is a cycled process, a cycle that is constantly recurring. Creativity is not something where you work on it, finish up, and you're done. From inventors and artists to CEOs of the Fortune 500, all of them share the quality of reflection and refinement when looking at their ideas, experiences, projects, or products.

We all have awesome ideas. Whether we have the confidence to develop them further is a matter of shifting our mindset. The problem is, once we invest in developing an idea, the work becomes more difficult. We wonder how long it will take to finish and consider scaling back the project. Sometimes we even reach that low point where we start thinking in those all-or-nothing terms of success and failure. We figure our only possible outcomes are total validation or utter humiliation, and there's no way we'll nail it the first time out, so why even try? We ditch the idea and leave it for someone else to tackle. Does this sound familiar? Absolutely. This self-defeating thought process is common, and we've all been there, but our awesome ideas don't have to end up this way. I wholeheartedly believe it's possible to overcome the doubt and fear and forge ahead into the unknown, even when failure is a distinct possibility. To achieve this, you need to hear the stories of others overcoming failure and adversity. You need to challenge your students to research and find their hero CEO, entrepreneur, or inventor, just like they can find that same heroism in a sports player, musician, or actor. Next is to engage in a small, challenge-based experience that lets failure be a moment that can be reflected upon and refined.

If we overcome this, we can surprise ourselves, experience unexpected outcomes, and beyond completing a project, realize that we learned a lot for next time. That is because making awesomeness is hard and long. If we fail or experience the unexpected, we will be ready for next time. And I cannot stress enough how important the next time is. In education we must shift our approach and value where experiences must be perfected in one shot, so we can move on to the next thing.

Let's get practical for a moment. I want to challenge you, as I do others in my workshops, to embark on a hands-on journey with me. We discussed the "Candle Problem," but what about other activities? If we're teaching a group of first graders, and matches and candles are not an option, what can we do? Some of these activities are inspired by others while some are my own. It all starts with a bag of LEGOs and a whole lot of imagination. Quite often, if I ask my workshop participants about their creativity and imagination, they might say they have none, but if I force them to be creative, magic happens. During a workshop on understanding learning styles, I had participants take a short learning style questionnaire. Each group sat at a table with a bag of LEGOs in the center. I invited participants to engage with the pieces, if they chose, as we discussed various insights into visual, auditory, and kinesthetic learning. Toward the end of the workshop, we focused again on the LEGOs and made note of different participants' use of the LEGOs. After scoring their own assessments, we discussed our own strengths, weaknesses, which surprised us the most, and why. What we discovered is that those with even the smallest amount of strength in the area of kinesthetic learning interfaced with the blocks in some fashion. Some organized them side by side, others made a simple stack, while others attempted to create something with them. LEGO has their own creative spin on this activity. The Build A Duck challenge is done with six blocks, four yellow and two red. The directions are simple; make a duck. The

pieces imply a straightforward approach, but what ensues is nothing short of extraordinary. Six LEGO pieces can produce more than twenty different variations and representations of "what is a duck." Did you use all the pieces? Are those flat pieces feet? Are they a beak? Are they wings? Are they even needed for someone else to know your duck is a duck? It's questions like these that stimulate creative thinking. Inspired by the LEGO activity and other divergent thinking experiences such as the paperclip challenge, I started to wonder "How Many Uses Does a LEGO Wheel Have?" The result is another fun way to introduce creative problem solving to students as they start to assemble "silly ideas," realizing that hidden among them is a really great one. It really pushes the creative potential as you try to "make it work" or, even better, discover a novel use for a LEGO wheel beyond transporting LEGO figurines around your LEGO world.

For students in the primary grades, working on problems and challenges with multiple answers and outcomes is a great way to encourage critical and non-linear thinking. The potential is that our students in the primaries will learn to experience something bigger than their own thinking and experiences early on, allowing for diverse perspectives and approaches to be welcome as they get older. For high school students, it's an effective way to demonstrate that creativity and innovation are complex social processes that require communication and collaboration.

Whenever I engage high school teachers in a discussion of collaboration, they generally view it as an elementary process. That is because they are confusing collaboration with cooperative learning. We all know the experience. Assign a group a project, expect all of them to do a percentage of all components, and grade them on the final product. This is not collaboration. Collaboration is about helping people work together to achieve an outcome that could not be achieved by an individual.

It's about helping people identify their strengths and watching how they can support one another as they work to solve the problem. This is the way that technology startups and many other successful businesses work. It isn't about who's in charge or most talented. It's about many talented and creative people helping one another refine their skills and contribute to a project or experience that is something greater than themselves. In today's world, we are more connected than ever before, and innovation is fueled by the connections we make beyond our four walls and community.

Running a Marathon

You wake up early with a feeling of excitement. Today is the Los Angeles Marathon, and you cannot wait to run the race! You're out of the gate running with such excitement, yet somewhere around mile three of twenty-six, your energy level drops. By mile seven, you're dragging and finally give up at mile ten. How could you have failed? You think to yourself that you're a horrible runner, a non-athlete, and won't ever succeed in running a marathon. This is a common scenario for many of the 25,000 participants. Our creative capacity, confidence, and courage are similar to a marathon. Why do some fail and give up? Why do some abandon the challenge altogether, never to run again? Did they train? How long? Did they plan? How much? Did they eat right? How often? Just like waking up the morning of a marathon and starting the race, creativity isn't something that you just start expressing and acting upon. It takes time and effort to develop a creative mindset. If you're guided, you can reveal an incredible creative potential we ALL have. When your mission is to help others and provide them with value, then your creative potential starts to thrive.

INNOVATION IS A COMPLEX SOCIAL PROCESS

COLLABORATION IS REQUIRED

Creating Value

As a designer, I was challenged daily to create value for companies. Whether it was a new logo, website, or a marketing campaign, it was my job to use media to connect with a company's customer base. I find myself looking back almost daily at those experiences when trying to design learning experiences for my students. My end goal is to develop students' skills and increase their knowledge, but the question is to do that in a way that is personal, engaging, and open-ended without sacrificing academic achievement. I believe we do that by giving students the opportunity to create value. We give them the tools, time, and space to create something that will serve a purpose, something that will have social value for someone else. Guide your students by encouraging them to ask these questions: Can others benefit from my work? Can others learn from it? Could others be inspired by it? For many

GIVE STUDENTS THE OPPORTUNITY TO CREATE VALUE.

educators, this area feels too fluid and murky and subjective, but this is where creativity resides, and it is up to us to teach our students how to be comfortable with this mindset.

One thing that drives creativity is the social impact of the outcome. When you look at the success of social media, it is rooted in the value created by social connections. It has flourished because of individualized relationships and the creative flow that connects them. Consider how users share content, whether it is a text, photo, or video, and how others respond, value, and engage with it. Then students come to school, put away their phones, and experience five to eight hours of isolated learning in siloed environments devoid of social connection. We need to learn how to take the creative experiences behind what makes social media such a success and make that part of the learning process and environment in our classrooms.

Twitter: Can you carry on a meaningful conversation? How about in 240 characters? This platform is a great example for students to develop their skills in concise and clear writing.

Instagram: Can you tell stories through photos? Do your curated visuals invite people to engage and come back to experience more?

YouTube: How we can we teach others? Video has dominated the ability for others to learn what were once complex tasks and skills. Today ANYONE can go to YouTube and learn thousands of different sought-after and important skills for the world of work.

A Messy Process

In today's education system, assembly-line learning still reigns supreme. While that model might have worked well in the nineteenth and twentieth centuries, the twenty-first century is going to require a more agile, adaptable, and creative approach to problem solving and work in general.

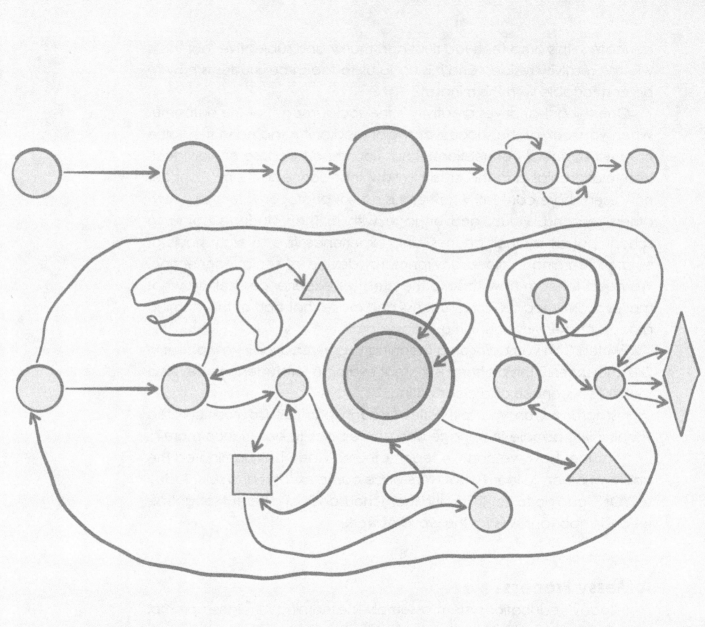

With advances in technology replacing the need to develop new skills and processes, creativity will become more important than ever before. One challenge I foresee is that educators—and countless other professionals—must accept that the creative process is super messy.

Creativity isn't a simple, linear, multistep process. It is wrought with steps back that are really steps forward and full of unknowns that need to be assessed as part of the process. In education we tend to gravitate toward known problems. Even in the sciences, where hypotheses and experimentation are meant to thrive, we still keep students in the realm of the tried, true, and expected. Offering students opportunities to engage with problems whose solutions are unknown or challenging students to discover problems that are unknown are great ways for students to see true creativity at work and watch their problem solving skills grow.

In the worlds of design and entrepreneurship, the unknown path is the status quo. External factors, unknowns, and the unexpected are all involved when considering creative approaches to problems, regardless of what type they may be.

Finding Purpose

Creativity is rooted in purpose, in the sense that without purpose, it is rather difficult to produce something creative. Take this book as an example. I found that the more I focused on how this book could help others, rather than simply sharing my expertise, the ideas flowed like a raging river as opposed to a trickling stream. Creativity requires you to develop a relationship with others. If you look at artists, musicians, and designers, their best work involves inviting others to be part of it, enjoy it, use it, and even question it. Creativity serves no purpose if it's locked up in your journal and kept private. The true creative drive comes from doing something that will benefit others.

Not All Artists Can Draw, Not All Drawers Are Artists

I once visited a friend's home and admired a large oil painting depicting some well-known Rabbinic figures. The style and detail of the painting was incredible, and it was one of those pieces you could sit and look at for hours, finding new details each time you observed it. I ran down my list of painters to discover who painted this incredible work of art. Each time his answer was no. What he said next surprised me; he said that it was an original replica, and it was painted by a group based in China. After doing some research, I was shocked to discover that there is an entire industry in China that teaches people to paint like a master, and the paintings are sold at a fraction of the cost that you might find at a New York art opening. This is just one of many stories of my journey and career as an artist, designer, and educator that really shook my perception of creativity and art and who holds the keys. It was then that I realized that all artists could be painters, but not all painters could be artists. That is because an artist expresses what's on the mind and the soul. That creative expression is built on three things:

1. The confidence to create
2. The will to create
3. The courage to have your creativity questioned

We need these three to reveal that creative capacity and not listen to the voices that question and doubt us. As I said before many times, that voice is in our head, but we cannot stop creating.

During my senior year of college, a professor told me that the rules have been established, and now I am free to break them.

The reason I became an educator was to cultivate creativity in my students and empower them to use that mindset to solve interesting problems in the world. In college I visited a friend at a prestigious art school and was shocked to see a student with a projector shining on a

ART EXPRESSES THE MIND AND THE SOUL

canvas painting away. While I admired their creative tracing solution, how could this be considered art? My friend laughed and said, "Art isn't about skill; it's about how you see the world." She then shared that her entire portfolio submission to get into art school consisted of a magazine collage canvas that she paint-traced over. The truth is, at the time, I was offended and began to be much more skeptical about art. I valued skill over vision, and it wasn't until I got accepted into the printmaking program at California State University, Long Beach, that I learned what art and creativity were all about. My head professor, Roxanne Sexauer, taught me that once you know the rules, you are ready to break them.

I was standing in front of a series of Albrecht Durer etchings, and I asked her if I would ever be able to draw like this. She said even if I gave up all entertainment and sat etching for ten hours a day, I would never achieve that level of skill. I was a little bummed at first but then realized what she was telling me—that creativity is individual because each of us sees the world in a distinctly different way, and that perspective informs everything we do in life. We all might be looking through similar binoculars, but what we see and choose to explore will vary greatly, depending on our unique experiences.

Those binoculars also give us much needed perspective—making some things appear closer than they are. Students need that because adults need that.

Creative Courage—Act on It!

This chapter is all about identifying the mindset of creativity. Dispelling the stereotypes surrounding creativity as a talent or experience is critical to shift your thinking. Overcoming the functional fixedness of the world around us is step two. Next is understanding how to search outside of our personal and professional lives for people who are successful and gain from their creative approaches. Finally we need to view collaboration and connectedness as a way to take that mindset into reality. So what are you waiting for? Choose your own adventure and go to chapter two.

- Do you consider yourself creative? Why or why not?
- Who are some of your creative heroes? What do you admire about their lives and work?
- Think of a project or idea or challenge you have always wanted to tackle. What holds you back? How could you shift your thinking to feel more confident about taking it on?
- How diverse is your professional life? Your personal life? How could you make it more diverse?
- Think of someone at your school or organization you've always wanted to work with. Try collaborating on an activity, event, or lesson and see what you can learn!

CHAPTER 2

FAILURE IS A STOP ON THE JOURNEY, NOT A DESTINATION

"A righteous one falls down seven times and gets up."
—Proverbs 24:16

"The way to succeed is to double your failure rate."
—Thomas Watson

There is a beloved acronym that has lodged itself into the collective vocabulary of education, and that is F.A.I.L.—First Attempt In Learning. I realize this term is meant to encourage the embracement of failure, but I find it to be limiting in one key area that makes a failed experienced a learned experience as well. That area is reflection. It is a significantly under focused skill that can equip students to learn to successfully pivot in the face of challenge. In education today, the notion of failure is a game-over moment where students are taught that not only does the failure represent who they are as a person, but their failure will also follow them via their permanent record. Outside of education, failure is not an outcome, but in fact, a first attempt. It is part of the process of reaching long-term success. Education focuses on the short-term, the unit, the lesson, which is why classroom learning tends to focus around creating planned experiences with clearly defined outcomes, such as fill in the blank or the answer is D. Real high-level thinking and complex problem solving do not exist in the land of multiple choice. In business, especially start-up culture, failing is not an intended outcome, nor is it planned for. It is the result of taking risks and going beyond the pale of "possible and expected." No worksheet, quiz, or cookie-cutter group project is possible here because the end goal is something bigger than that, its inception complex, multi-faceted, and difficult to define. As a result of this level of challenge, it is not just a "first attempt in learning;" it is F.A.I.L.U.R.E., which transforms it into a first attempt that will lead to additional and potentially unnecessary and avoidable attempts Unless Reflection Exists.

Failure is such a funny conversation. On one side, we have students who are terrified of failure and view anything less than perfection as a game-over experience. I once had a student (who actually deserved a B) beg me to change his A- to an A because his parents were down his throat about his GPA. What if I had changed it? In the short-term, it

might have helped the kid. In the long-term, he might have graduated from an Ivy League school, experienced his first real failure in life, and collapsed into a cocoon of depression and helplessness. (That is a true story, by the way. I have a friend who got fired from his job after gliding through school and ended up spending thousands of dollars on therapy and life coaching.)

On the other side of the failure conversation are teachers who are like, "Yeah, failure rocks! Let's fail, fail often, and fail forward." Believe it or not, there is a very productive middle where you look at failure as part of a journey and not a destination. You use it as a conversation piece, and you reflect on how to improve. School is a great time for those experiences because there is less at stake. It's a time to help you value the opinions of others but learn to not let them rule over you or, even worse, need them to feel validation as a person.

I want to share an awesome failure with you because this book is full of what I hope is great and practical advice that I myself need to take.

I failed.

I tried to launch a podcast in 2016 and went about it all wrong. Looking back, it is actually a little funny, but in the midst of it, I was frustrated and felt like I let a lot of people down, especially the guest I had on the show. Years ago, I got into Gary Vaynerchuk. His books were awesome, and his podcast—*The GaryVee Audio Experience*—was even better. So when I launched the Educated By Design project and began to scale various mediums, I figured what better way to start than by naming the podcast the "Educated By Design Audio Experience." Then I bought an intro and outro bumper on Fiverr, the world's largest freelancing marketplace, that had my voice introducing the podcast in a style similar to him, and I was ready to go! From the very beginning, I struggled to get guests and then struggled with the whole scope and sequence of how to record, edit, and distribute the content. It was just not working I only released one episode. I recorded a second episode, but never released it because I just couldn't keep up with the pace I had set. I also felt horrible that someone took the time to be interviewed by me and that I never released that episode. Eventually, I sat down to figure out how and why the project didn't work. I used a quasi-design thinking approach, and I realized that my empathy approach was off-base. I wasn't designing with a user in mind, I was designing what I thought people wanted. I had to reflect on the following: What problem was I trying to solve? Why was it a problem for my audience? Who was my audience? I wanted to connect teachers with creative professionals who would share their journeys and the approaches they took to succeed. My hope was that teachers would gain insights and learn new strategies and activities to develop their own creative confidence and help nurture the same in their students.

So why didn't it work? I had missed an important step: Purpose. Not my own purpose but the purpose for my audience. Why would teachers want to be more creative? Do they view their lack of creativity as an obstacle to achieve a specific goal? Why would teachers want to employ creative strategies in their classrooms? I believe that, for most educators, the reason is their students. As educators, a huge part of our lives is about our students and their success.

I sat down with one of my students and decided to create a podcast to help students develop their own creative confidence and figure out how to succeed beyond the test. I shared this idea with teachers in my PLN, and they were thrilled. In just a few weeks, the guest list grew from three booked guests to fifteen. The roster included former vice presidents at Apple, senior directors at Snapchat, executives at Twitch, and evangelists at Amazon. Each guest shared incredible insights into their success. The common threads? There were many, but the one that fits here is that these creative professionals treated failure as a moment to think and regroup. None of them viewed failure as a game-over experience or something to spend more than a few moments or days grappling with. When I asked those guests how they overcame the failure so quickly, they said they weren't in the habit of allowing their setbacks to define them. Their view was that they didn't fail—their project failed. And that wasn't just some breezy concept or lip service. These people went on to back up that attitude with action, fixing what had failed. I love that! Why aren't we teaching our students to approach failure in this way?

In our current education system, anything below a C—universally seen as average—is essentially considered an F. Above average and excellent are within the reach of anyone who can memorize and cram for a standardized test. Like most narrow, performance-based models, our system doesn't truly assess a student's mastery or authentic learning. Instead, it conditions both teachers and students to internalize failure and allow it to define their overall ability to learn, teach, and thrive. In the real world, however, this obsession with high-level performance and compliance will get you very little, and at the advancement rate of technology today, the jobs that do require such skills will be almost obsolete by 2020. When discussing this aspect of our education system, I am reminded of a wry quote, "Everybody is a genius. But if you judge a fish by its ability to climb a tree, it will live its whole life believing that it is stupid."

Innovation Takes Time

The word innovation today is flashy. Everyone wants to be innovative, and you would be hard-pressed to find someone who doesn't want to innovate. The challenge is that truly innovative products or practice takes time. They aren't a two-day project or a week-long experiment. True innovation requires all parties involved to really invest themselves in the process and believe that the effort is for something significant. This

EVERYBODY IS A GENIUS. BUT IF YOU JUDGE A FISH BY ITS ABILITY TO CLIMB A TREE, IT WILL LIVE ITS WHOLE LIFE BELIEVING THAT IT IS STUPID.

-Albert Einstein

gives us the ability to teach our students to think about failure differently because now it has a purpose; we must eventually turn the conversation to the inherent value of taking intellectual and professional risks. As educators, we must model confident and willful creativity for our students. Ultimately, we have to show them it's right and acceptable to pursue ideas, projects, and ventures that may well result in failure but that could also result in significant advancement. And a big part of that lesson is making sure they know that major breakthroughs are rarely achieved on the first try.

True innovation requires us to view failure as one of multiple stepping stones that will lead to success. It is with this understanding that our imaginations can thrive and begin to craft creative solutions to the problems we face. I'm not saying we should teach our students to expect to fail, but I do believe they should know it's a natural and organic part of the creative process. Consider some of our earliest accomplishments in life—standing, learning to walk, tying shoes, and riding a bicycle. Very few of us learn to do any of those things the first time around. Fast forward a couple of decades to launching a tech startup, getting into medical school, or passing the bar, and it's the same story. First-time success simply isn't the norm—and that's okay.

The problem is that many of us can't shake the letter-grade mindset that drained so much of our confidence, wonder, and creativity. We spent twelve or more years cramming and memorizing to get it right the first time, every time. And when we didn't—even when we scored a C—we were conditioned to considered ourselves failures. It is as if there were only two types of grades, an A and anything lower than that is on par with an F.

Why is it so difficult to innovate on the first try? I believe it's because true innovation requires the innovator to develop a solution or product that creates value for others. Simply put, the best outcome needs to be reviewed, revised, and reflected upon with the expectation that the first iteration will not be the best. Now try to fit that approach into our current educational system. Imagine if learning in our schools started with teachers saying, "I don't know" or "I wonder," instead of the careful conversation designed to ensure that they're seen as masters of their classroom content. While a complete overhaul of our educational system might not be possible via your classroom, there is room for teachers to teach students about the inherent value of failure and its role in the creative process. Whether you consider Edison the sole inventor of the lightbulb, to understand what true innovation looks like, it's important to understand that Edison was not trying to invent the lightbulb. He was trying to give people the ability to see in the dark.

SHAKE THE LETTER-GRADE MINDSET

Failure Can Empower

I believe it was Edison's end goal, his creative will to change the world for the better, that fueled him to fail more than a thousand times as he worked toward a safe and sustainable light source. It's that kind of failure—along with the understanding that first does not always mean best—that can embolden and empower our students.

I often wish I had been taught as a child that failure makes you stronger. Children, particularly during their preschool years, fail all the time, but they don't think about it in those terms. They are not cognizant of it.

They learn to walk, ride bikes, mimic Mary Poppins with an umbrella off a ten-foot, high wall (Okay, I was recently informed that not everyone did that growing up.), get up, dust themselves off, and keep going. What freedom! Then, sadly, they start school, become immersed in linear learning experiences with calculated outcomes, and learn to play it safe. I would argue that Failure 101 needs to be a prerequisite to middle school. Students need to be challenged in a way that they are guaranteed to fail, discuss and reflect on it, and grow from it. When you look at the social environment of today's youth, it revolves around experiences that promote empowerment through failure. Whether it's playing the latest video game, struggling to get 100 likes on your social feed, or excelling in sports, our youth have a chance to view failure as an investment in long-term, high-level success. They can come to understand that failure is simply another learning opportunity—an opportunity to regroup, take a breath, and review what went wrong. And unlike Wile E. Coyote, take time to read the writing on the wall.

So let's ditch the participant trophies and easy mode and give students an opportunity to empower themselves through experiences that require them to give 100 percent and then some. I'm not talking about grit or rigor (Google those terms to find some good books on the subject.), just old-fashioned hard work and patience.

Failure Is Reflective

We leave almost zero time for reflection in education today. Outside of our students sitting and wondering why they didn't get at least 90 percent on a big test, they aren't given the space and time for reflection because it's not measurable in the traditional sense. Even worse, many educators view reflection as a soft skill that shouldn't take up time during school. But reflection is a critical part of succeeding after the

failure, and failure is a critical part of learning. I firmly believe students who learn the skill of reflection will be better equipped not only for academic setbacks but also for personal and social setbacks. It's certainly a skill they could use later in life, especially if they are able to retain their creative drive.

In the world of business, there are companies that thrive by taking risks and making decisions that include a failure scenario. Those companies outlive their content, complacent, and play-it-safe competitors. Imagine what the world would look like if we gave students the same types of open spaces and opportunities that companies like Google, Edmunds, and Tesla do? One scenario is that our students develop a confidence and appreciation for failed experiences. The other scenario is that we give our students opportunities to discover how to be a linchpin in the work they love, whether they start their own company or work for one. For failure to become an asset, we need to give them tangible and real experiences. Failure can't take the form of a physics exam; it must be a model rocket launch that needs to hit or land on a target. Then failure doesn't become detestation but a stage to achieve a goal. Whether it is computer programing, engineering, visual communication, or grant writing, a clear goal and opportunities exist to keep improving till we succeed. What ends up making reflection essential is being able to ask ourselves tough questions and being humble enough to answer them honestly.

So how do we reflect? Well, first you need to believe that the first or second attempt isn't your best. Do you have time for more? If not, that's fine, and let's be clear: We are not planning to fail, nor are we saying that failure is appropriate for all experiences. As a father, I struggle with standing on the side and watching my kids do things that they might fail at or struggle with. Still, as much as it hurts, I know they will be stronger and better from the struggle than if I do it for them.

Failure is part of big ideas. It means that you need to embrace the unknown and understand that risk is required. We aren't talking about learning 2+2. We are talking about understanding how to face challenges where x+y=z, and all three are truly unknown.

Airbnb launched three times before they became the household name of home sharing and travel accommodations. Imagine if they closed shop the second time. How did they do it? An article from *GrowthHackers* put it bluntly as "'Pure Unadulterated Hustle' in the Face of Initial Resistance." Failure is only as good as your confidence in yourself, your team, your work, and your mission.

Elon Musk is another example of someone who is no stranger to failure. While not many of us will ever have the chance to launch a rocket, let alone crash one, his company, SpaceX, crashed over ten rockets, trying to create the first-ever self-landing rocket. This event was a feat that not only cost millions to perfect but also nearly bankrupted the company on their last failed launch.

When failure is standardized, the results are game-over. When failure is part of a nonlinear complex process, then reflection and refinement create outcomes that are more meaningful and much richer in quality. It's the complex and nonlinear challenges that our students will, without question, face the day after graduating college. It might not be a startup; it might be as simple as figuring out how to manage your monthly expenses, but that first failure, the experience they have been taught to avoid, will be a painful one.

We Aren't Our Failures

Bottom line? Failure isn't pleasant. I recently had some pushback to my view of failure. The person questioned why I was choosing to place so much emphasis on failure. Naturally, I pushed right back, questioning why we avoid it and pretend it doesn't exist. I understand that failure is a topic that can make people uncomfortable, but it's part of life. That's not changing anytime soon. I believe the important thing to remember is that failure is an occurrence. It's something that happens. It isn't who we are, and it doesn't define us. *We aren't failures.* We make decisions and calculations that might be off, and that means something needs to be reworked. Elon Musk once said, "If things are not failing, *you're* not innovating enough." Look at his words closely. If *things* aren't failing, you're not innovating enough. It's all about emphasis, and it's all about mindset. Fail fast, fail often, but fail smart, and please don't make it your Algebra 2 final.

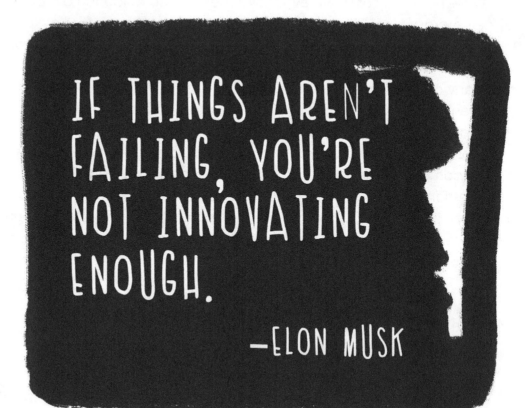

IF THINGS AREN'T FAILING, YOU'RE NOT INNOVATING ENOUGH.

—ELON MUSK

Fail Fast, Fail Forward

This chapter is more about embracing failure than teaching others how to overcome their encounters with failure. Remember, we are not talking about a problem with a clear answer! Failure in that respect might just be poor planning, lack of effort, or carelessness. While those are *also* great learning experiences, the failure above is something that might happen two, three, or even eight times in different capacities because the big idea is there, and you and those around you are hungry to achieve success beyond a fill-in-the-blank, bubbled letter learning outcome.

- Think of a time you failed. What were you attempting? How did it feel to fail? What was your response to that failure?
- What have you learned about failure over the years?
- How do you help your students understand and experience failure? What are the challenges you face in teaching them about failure?
- What are some activities or lessons you can tackle in your classroom to help your students better understand that failure is part of the creative process?

CHAPTER 3

EMPATHY INSPIRES CREATIVITY

Unless two people are on the "same wavelength," the empathy which one shows to the other does not really leave sufficient encouragement to be a healing influence.
—Or HaChaim

When you show deep empathy toward others, their defensive energy goes down, and positive energy replaces it. That's when you can get more creative in solving problems.
—Stephen Covey

I learned early on that if I was going to be a successful designer and keep my sanity along the way, I needed to view the client as king. The saying goes, "The client is always right." It doesn't mean that they're actually right, but because you value their relationship, you are open to ensuring that they have the best experience regardless. As an educator, I know we all have our days, that one student pushes that one button and then BAM! We are human; we have our moments, but our gold standard has to be modeled after the service industry. The question is how? For starters, survey your students more. What are their interests? What are their values? In my Entrepreneur Studio course, I have students fill out a self-assessment survey. For many, this starts as a miserable and frustrating experience because they are not used to having a teacher ask them what they are interested in or what is important. I have had students complain that I am not just "telling them what to do" for an innovation project! It's a lot easier to be "wrong" and have happy and engaged customers, aka students who will be more inclined to share their great experiences with others, than to do damage control in the spirit of being right.

What does this attitude stem from? What triggers this move to make someone else's needs the priority? The answer is empathy. Empathy is one of those buzzwords that I hope never falls out of fashion. Feeling empathy is one of the most powerful abilities one can possess. It's the ability to truly understand and experience another person's feelings and concerns, and it's absolutely critical to personal and professional success. Without empathy, creative types can surely innovate, but they might lack the personal relationships that foster ideas like Amazon, Google, Lyft, and Airbnb. Now rather than start with empathy, many startups are riding on the back of the success of empathy while lacking empathy themselves. I could be wrong, but I think we might look back on the Uber for dog walking and shake our head a little bit. So how

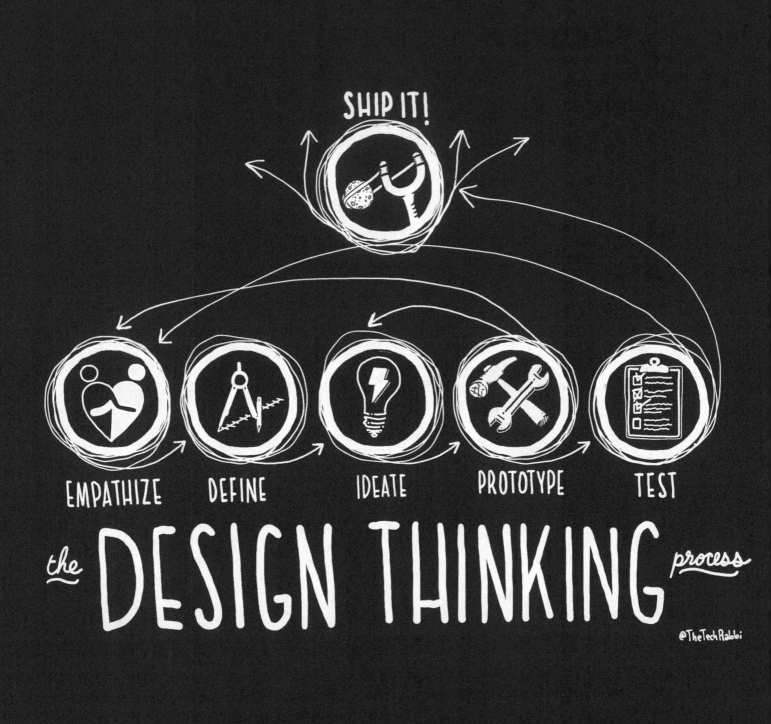

do we become more empathic? How do we introduce empathy to others? Most of all, how do we ensure that our students graduate with empathy as not just a vocabulary word but a way of living?

To answer this, we need to look at the role of empathy in the creative process. A great way to incorporate empathy and a student-first mentality is to create a classroom mission statement for the beginning of the year. A mission statement is not just what a company is all about; it is a reminder to all employees and customers what the company is supposed to represent, even when the times are tough. By tapping into your students' minds and collaborating with them, there is an opportunity for voices to be heard, buy-in to be had, and energy to be invested in making sure the mission is fulfilled. Take a look at some of the more well-known companies of today. How many mission statements below are you familiar with?

- Amazon: "To be Earth's most customer-centric company where people can find and discover anything they want to buy online."
- IKEA: "To create a better everyday life for the many people."
- TED: "Spread ideas."
- JetBlue: "To inspire humanity—both in the air and on the ground."
- Tesla: "To accelerate the world's transition to sustainable energy."

SURVEY YOUR STUDENTS MORE

Although I see empathy and creativity as an inseparable experience, the Design Thinking model crafted by Stanford and IDEO uses empathy as the springboard for their problem-solving methodology and, for most, puts empathy on the map.

The reason empathy is so valuable as a start of any process is because it places emphasis on people rather than product. Consider our classrooms and classrooms around the world. Are we designing learning experiences for people or for products? For test scores? For 3.0+ GPAs? Or for people who will grow up to be successful, passionate, and lovers of learning?

Empathy is the linchpin of the creative process, plain and simple. When we look at innovation, invention, and impact throughout history, it has always started with the desire to help others and make an impact.

EMPATHY IS THE LINCHPIN OF THE CREATIVE PROCESS, PLAIN AND SIMPLE.

Design Starts with how you look at it. To influence what you do with it.

@TheTechRabbi

Take Edison, for example. Whether you are on Team Edison in the race to harness the power of electricity or not, his story is legendary. His famous quote, stating that he "had not failed, but discovered 10,000 ways that don't work," is certainly food for thought.

For me, I see something more powerful in his work and what drove and inspired him to change the course of human history. I don't think that Edison was trying to invent the lightbulb. I believe he was trying to invent the ability for the world to see in the dark. How is such a passion developed? Sure, the dream of being a famous inventor could have been a driving force, but we all possess the desire and potential to impact those around us. Empathy is what allows us to be positive, personal, and concerned with the success of others. The most successful companies and startups in history have a mission that puts people before their product or service. Look no further than Apple, Google, Amazon, Tesla, Uber, and Airbnb. My favorite story, beyond those working on the next big thing in a garage, is the Airbnb story. It illustrates the power of empathy so beautifully.

Airbnb evolved from a problem. Booking a hotel at major conferences is difficult, risky, and above all, expensive. A hotel near a conference center might jack up prices 200 percent, block off rooms to create more of a demand, and leave you with no place to stay. This happens to me, time and time again, at the ISTE conference, no matter what I do, and many years, I find myself at an awesome Airbnb. The Airbnb I booked at ISTE's 2017 conference even came with a Mastiff puppy in a pen as part of the package. So Airbnb, you see, wanted to solve this problem and decided to create a "Bed and Breakfast" with some "air" mattresses in their apartment to address this need for a Bay Area conference. Do you see where I am going with this? Airbnb was born out of a significant challenge for people, including themselves. It took Airbnb a lot more than empathy to launch a $20-billion-dollar company

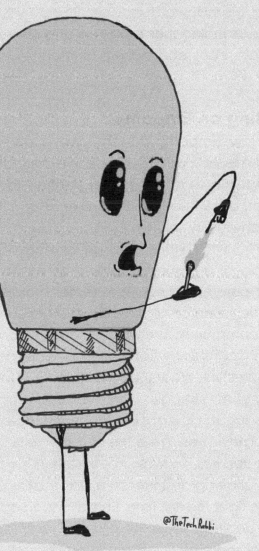

in less than five years, but I honestly believe that empathy is what rocketed them toward success. Empathy is about looking at people and understanding their problems and challenges. It is also about the desire to help, heal, and make a difference.

Acting on Empathy

Now empathy has to have a disclaimer. It cannot come at the expense of overall success. We cannot put everything into empathy and try to then develop a solution that isn't sustainable. Empathy is great, but without common sense and intelligence, you will not create a high-quality solution.

Years ago, I took a Design Thinking MOOC from Stanford. They shared a story of a group set to help an African community with water loss in their cisterns during the summer months. Their solution—a lightweight, plastic reservoir that could be buried—was completely rejected by the community. This was their segue into empathy, because the group didn't consider what materials were part of the community's culture and lifestyle. What they didn't show is how they resolved the challenge. One of my struggles with the Design Thinking model as a designer and an educator is that it inadvertently segregates the "steps," implying that empathy ends. While this isn't their intention, I see the model discussed and applied this way. In education it's due to the systemic problem of school being designed in a way that results in everything needing to be done right the first time. Empathy can actually be more significant once you begin to solve the problem and then engage with those in need rather than test a prototype product or solution.

I want to highlight the power of empathy by sharing a personal story. As an education technology trainer, I have had the opportunity to deliver a fairly significant number of workshops and other professional development experiences. In designing workshops, I send out a pre-survey, aimed at getting to know participants, their passions, and their visions for their professional growth. Sometimes I am able to have a conference call to get even more detail. Why do I do this? I do it because walking into a school and claiming I have all kinds of cutting-edge technology and the expertise to transform the teaching and learning in their classrooms is a terrible idea. Where is the empathy in that? My mission as a trainer and facilitator is to empower educators to feel confident and capable of utilizing technology in their classrooms in a meaningful and sustainable way. Notice that my expertise and cutting-edge tech are not part of the mission.

To successfully design professional development workshops, participants need to feel they are viewed as a professional. As a trainer, workshops must be developed with a sense of empathy and compassion for faculty. You must understand their needs, the school culture, the challenges they face with access to resources, support, and above all, time and expectations. I would argue that the same is true for any manager, administrator, or director, no matter the organization. For any professional supervising a team of workers, it's critical that they know you value them as people and employees and care about their hopes and the challenges they face.

In 2014, I wanted to help a third-grade class learn a little bit about empathy. A colleague and I designed a project in which students

VALUE YOUR TEAM AS PEOPLE. CARE ABOUT THEM.

would do research on a specific topic that would be digitally published. Their work would be used as a resource for the rest of the class to learn from and gain a general understanding of the topic. Allowing students to facilitate their own learning is no innovation of mine, but the way in which I packaged the experience for the students was something special. When we asked students how they learn best, they were very open. Some shared that they liked audio, many preferred video and photos, and others liked using their hands. Learning styles aside, it was a nice moment of students learning about themselves, but one particular rephrasing of the question left the room in silence:

"How do you think others learn best, and how could you help them learn?"

The words, "I like" and "that works for me" were out the window, and the students didn't know how to proceed. That is the moment you want to have. That's the moment empathy enters the creative process. When people are stuck and full of uncertainty, they begin to look around at the challenges and frustrations other people are experiencing. It's the moment where learning gets awesome. In the end, those students solved it, mastered it, and engaged their peers. Everyone was so immersed in the learning that recess was passed up by more than half the class. And it all started with one little word.

Empathy.

Be Empathically Aware

As I said before, empathy doesn't simply end during the design process, but there needs to be a point where you are ready to move on and develop the product or solution further. To reach that point, I think you have to answer these key questions. (Keep in mind the energy and diversity of the groups you are working with.)

WHAT IS THE CULTURE OF
THE GROUPS OF PEOPLE LIKE?

WHAT ARE THEIR VALUES?

WHAT ARE THEIR STRUGGLES AS A GROUP
(AND AS INDIVIDUALS IF POSSIBLE)?

WHAT RESOURCES DO THEY HAVE AVAILABLE?

WHAT IS THEIR HISTORY OF
EMBRACING CHANGE?

WHAT LEVELS OF COLLABORATION AND SOCIAL
CONNECTEDNESS EXIST IN THE GROUP?

The oversimplification of empathy to understanding and sharing the feelings of another is only as strong as how well you know the other person or group. You might feel you are empathizing with a struggle, but based on the background information that you lack, your solution might fail. As a designer, I struggled with this regularly, as I needed to answer the questions above about clients and their client base as well. To support someone, service them, design for them, and teach them, you have to know them intimately, and for many, that is unfamiliar and uncomfortable. Remember, you have not even defined or attempted to ideate a solution to the problem. You can't until you truly understand the other to solve it in a way that they would solve it themselves if they only had your experience and expertise.

I think it is important to point out that empathy should not be at the expense of your own identity or the confidence you should have in your thoughts and opinions. Empathy doesn't mean letting people push you around or intimidate you into conforming to their way of thinking. What it should do is give you a new perspective that helps you better understand another person's behavior.

A Gamer's Story

I am not sure how evergreen the legacy of *Fortnite* is, but it is safe to say that almost anyone reading this has at least heard of *Fortnite*. If gaming history gives us any clues, you can expect this game to only increase in popularity. At a recent conference, I asked a group of two hundred educators what they thought about *Fortnite* and its role in education. What if we used the game as a medium to empower students to do research, write authentic, high-quality content, and present their findings to an audience? It could be a fun way to leverage empathy and students to get the output you want in those foundational literacy areas. Having students run surveys and then use their math skills to analyze and assess their data and findings are good ways to teach students the power of the scientific method. The idea is pretty out there and the audience reaction was a mix of laughter and curiosity. Teaching statistics and presentation skills through *Fortnite* might not replace curriculum, but it can definitely serve as a passion project for students. Creativity is about seeing the connections between two unrelated things. Finding a way to bridge the gap between Common Core and other foundational skills with *Fortnite* could be considered creative thinking. What makes it even more powerful is that this is what empathy is all about: helping with a challenge from the vantage point of another person!

When we find a way to relate to them, students are open to understanding how the academic skills and knowledge they spend all day engaging in may fulfill the age-old question of "when will I ever use this?" Take writing, for example. My students don't believe me that writing is the core of all strong and successful communication skills. So I went on Twitter and tweeted out the following question to Brandon Steiner, a successful businessman and investor:

Brandon Steiner ✔ @BrandonSteiner · May 7
Ask me anything!

💬 16   🔁 3   ♡ 3   ✉

Rabbi Michael Cohen ✔ @TheTechRabbi · May 7
What is the single most important skill that high school students should be working on beyond aquiring knowledge and being tested on it?

💬 1   🔁   ♡ 1   ılı

Brandon Steiner ✔
@BrandonSteiner

[Following]

Replying to @TheTechRabbi

Writing is essential. If you believe communication is a key ingredient to being successful, last time I checked writing has a big part in that.

9:55 AM - 7 May 2018

Then it dawned on me. Most students don't start school with a dislike of reading and writing. Their disdain for it comes from years of being forced to do it on someone else's terms. On occasion I get to teach a ten-week creative writing seminar for eighth graders at a local school. I always start the class with a simple question:

WHY DO YOU HATE WRITING?

Nine times out of ten, they say it's because they are forced to read and write about topics their teacher has selected. It's a serious reality, and I was part of that nine out of ten when I was in school. I never thought I would find my own voice in writing, let alone be a writer and author by trade. When we use empathy to help our students find their voices, we give them a real chance at mastering the critical skills to succeed in life.

Empathy in Practice

Empathy Mapping is a great way to practice employing empathy toward others and yourself (Sometimes we are our biggest critics!).

Challenge your students to use the following Empathy Map by scanning the QR code below.

This empathy map will help them discover the power of empathy beyond "what people do."

An Empathy List is a great way of documenting behavior that is rooted in kindness to best understand how empathy can better help us engage with and help those around us. Use the QR code below to access an Empathy List example.

Building this list weekly or monthly challenges our students to build not just empathy but reflection too. What other adjectives can you come up with?

Name: _____

Complete the sentences below by sharing how you and/or someone else successfully engaged in empathetic type behavior. If you have questions about one of the setences please ask a classmate or teacher.

This week I was:

kind by: _____

_____

caring by: _____

_____

helpful by: _____

_____

selfless by: _____

_____

patient by: _____

_____

thoughtful by: _____

_____

respectful by: _____

_____

This week someone was:

kind by: _____

_____

caring by: _____

_____

helpful by: _____

_____

selfless by: _____

_____

patient by: _____

_____

thoughtful by: _____

_____

respectful by: _____

_____

CHAPTER 4

COLLABORATION IS A PREREQUISITE FOR INNOVATION

It's the small acts that you do on a daily basis that turn two people from a "you and I" into an "us."
—The Lubavitcher Rebbe

Great things in business are never done by one person; they're done by a team of people.
—Steve Jobs

Hillel says, "If I am not for myself, who will be for me? But if I am only for myself, who am I? If not now, when?" Ethics of the Fathers, 1:14. For me, this quote from Hillel created one of those life-changing moments. In 2007, I was sitting with a Rabbi trying to make sense of these words. No matter what I said, it did not satisfy the Rabbi's question around the deeper meaning of this statement. He then shared with me something that I try to live with every single day. I believe it is a core of creative practice and promotes an incredible level of collaboration. The Rabbi proceeded to fill in the blanks between words to expand this quote into something powerful.

If I am not actively trying to help and provide good **for myself, who will be for me?** Is it my parents? My teachers? My friends? **But if I am** so self-absorbed and put all efforts into ensuring that success is **only for**

THE DAYS OF SOLO INNOVATION ARE LONG GONE, AND IT IS IMPERATIVE THAT WE TEACH THE NEXT GENERATION NOT TO SIMPLY COOPERATE AND WORK NICELY TOGETHER BUT TO AUTHENTICALLY COLLABORATE.

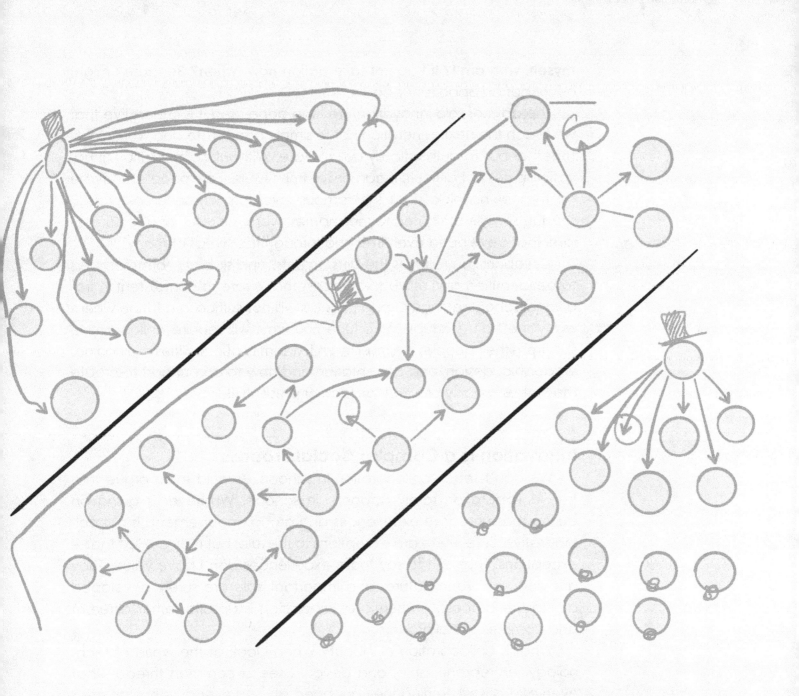

myself, who am I? If I do **not** take action **now, when?** Because I might never get an opportunity again.

The days of solo innovation are long gone, and it is imperative that we teach the next generation not to simply cooperate and work nicely together but to authentically collaborate. Without collaboration, innovation is not just difficult; it can prove impossible. Few people innovate on their own. Think of all the famous inventors whose breakthrough products, while attributed to their names, were the result of a social process that developed over time and through the sweat of many.

Collaboration requires the gifts, talents, and skills of team members to be identified and utilized, a process that is rare to nonexistent in traditional school settings. Group projects will not suffice in a future where everyone from startups to Fortune 500 firms will require collaborative skills from their people. We must learn to identify our qualities in planning, leadership, design, and presentation and how to do our part to create the highest quality product, project, or presentation.

Innovation Is a Complex Social Process

We don't teach collaboration in schools. I would even argue that true collaboration rarely happens in schools. Whatever is going on during those creative experiences and group engagements is not collaborative. Sure, there are exceptions to the rule, but they are just that—exceptions. That isn't to say those experiences don't have value. They are cooperative in nature, and important skills are surely developed during the process. Authentic collaboration is an altogether different and complex social process.

What is collaboration all about? When I look at the world of technology, entrepreneurship, and design, I see a common thread—that everyone has something they are good at, and everyone has an area

THE DAYS OF SOLO INNOVATION ARE LONG GONE

where they can grow. Collaboration is not just about a final product; it is about the experience, the social interaction, and the way in which minds, personalities, and abilities interface. Let's contrast the standard group project in a K–20 setting with that of a technology startup.

In a K–20 classroom, the project is assigned with clear expectations surrounding the content and integrity of the project, and group members are required to share the workload. In reality, most of the work is completed by a small number of group members or even one particularly driven and conscientious student. Over at the tech startup, a typical group project launches with a project manager, designer, software developer, marketing guru, quality assurance specialist, and content writer. All of these individuals have a clear understanding of their specialties. They own and take responsibility for their section of the project.

In this kind of setting, true collaboration shines. Not many companies can achieve this. Can you imagine duplicating this process in your classroom? It isn't easy and there is a potential for failure. When learning outcomes or *Cough!* test scores *Cough!* are at stake, it is hard to take risks. But imagine how powerful learning could be if this collaborative approach was taken seriously in schools. Collaboration is about building on the ideas of others and seeing those ideas as critical to the collective success and outcome of the group's efforts.

In a classroom setting, collaboration can be especially beneficial to students who have yet to fully understand their abilities or value the skills they do possess. Collaborative learning goes beyond content acquisition to touch on mentorship and soft skill building. You can certainly achieve cognitive development from memorization, but information is only as valuable as its application and use. Giving kids the space to develop actual abilities? That's priceless. So how do we turn typical classroom group work into true collaboration? We have to help students develop an understanding of different roles. Teamwork isn't about each team member taking on the same or equal load. It's about team mem bers taking on roles that suit their individual skills and talents and understanding those roles are critical to the outcome. Depending on their skills, some team members might bear a greater burden than others.

Let me share a story of an eighth-grade class that had a chance to understand and experience true collaboration. Each year this class takes a week-long science trip to Olympic National Park in upstate Washington, one of the only locations in the world to have tide pools, rainforests, and mile-high mountain tops all accessible within a few hours of driving. In years past, students experienced nature firsthand and documented it in their science notebook, compiling their thoughts from observations, expert guided tours, and experiments. After my first year of chaperoning this trip, I felt that the documentation process of the trip could use a revamp. The premise of the project was to take an antiquated approach to experiential learning and turn it into something meaningful not just for students but for others as well.

So during my second year of chaperoning the trip, I challenged my colleague, a veteran teacher of thirty years, to consider the role that technology could play in the way our students experience this spectacular park. We decided to propose that our students create a short nature documentary. This process would not just require them to be meticulous in documenting interesting and important scientific findings but to also research, plan, film, design, and produce a meaningful story. The final outcome would not only show their teacher they understood the various biospheres, flora, and fauna but also be something that others could consume to learn about this incredible place. It would also give them an opportunity to experience authentic collaboration. To be safe, students would still make use of their antiquated journals to ensure that all evidence of learning was documented, just in case the media experiment failed. Remember: always have a backup for big projects like these. Just don't emphasize it as a backup, to ensure students are engaged in the project with a potentially higher quality outcome.

When brainstorming this project, I wanted to ensure that I was thoughtful of the main goal of the trip and did my best to design an experience that still challenged students to compile accurate and relevant scientific content. To achieve this, I had to view those journals as more than pages of scripted fill-in-the-blank assignments. Rather, these journals contained the ingredients for incredible expression and inspiration that could convert into a medium that would bring others value. To achieve this, we presented students with several roles: a scriptwriter, three camera operators, a director, and an editor. Students understood that they needed to support each other, but their roles were critical in the success of the project.

My challenge now was to transform this from a group work-oriented project into an authentic collaborative experience that would separate this from just people working together to finishing a series of generic tasks.

The challenge with developing "collaborative experiences" is that we can fool ourselves into thinking that putting together groups of people intrinsically leads to them leveraging skills and supporting each other. In the cast of this nature documentary, it means that the scriptwriter writes scripts exclusively, or worse, *everyone* writes. Rather, *everyone*

should contribute to the writing processes but give the gifted writer of the group a chance to shine.

So I look to the world to see who is setting the pace for incredible experiences. That's when I find myself looking at Silicon Valley and the companies that, in many ways, are scripting the future with technology. That is when I need to ensure that my empathy lens is in full force because not everything in Mountain View is scalable and appropriate in the world of teaching and learning. Startup culture is becoming, and in some circles, already has become the next glamorized trend in education, and in many cases, for the wrong reasons. While that conversation is for a different time, there is one powerful lesson to be learned from the Startup Space, and that is that everyone brings their unique skills to the table, but more importantly, everyone is involved in ensuring the success and growth of other team members. *That is collaboration.*

As the trip progressed, I observed students looking for creative ways to capture nature, science experiments, and interesting observations. Whether it was the student dunking their iPad in a plastic bag in the water (with permission, of course!!!) or others taking stop motion footage of a walk through a temperate rainforest, the students were thinking beyond fill-in-the-blank learning and trying to create something meaningful and interesting. From beginning to end, they felt there was a *purpose* to their mission beyond journal writing and busy work. They believed someone was going to watch their short film, enjoy it, and even learn something new. This new and unfamiliar component of learning challenged students to up their game in all areas, resulting in a few students learning how to use Final Cut Pro, a professional video editing suite, because they were so inspired by the idea that this could be a medium that could boost the quality of what they wanted to share with others.

The challenge with collaboration is that it isn't an overnight success. It takes years to develop that level of awareness not just of self, but of

THE CHALLENGE WITH COLLABORATION IS THAT IT ISNT AN OVERNIGHT SUCCESS. IT TAKES YEARS TO DEVELOP THAT LEVEL OF AWARENESS NOT JUST OF SELF, BUT OF OTHERS. IT REQUIRES YOU TO KNOW YOUR STRENGTHS AND ACKNOWLEDGE YOUR WEAKNESSES.

others. It requires you to know your strengths and acknowledge your weaknesses. Such a way of thinking is not natural or instinctive, which is why you can have fifteen year olds and fifty year olds unable to tell you what they're passionate about, what they're good at, or how they can help others succeed and grow. I believe it is without question the role of schools to introduce and nurture these mission-critical soft skills starting in early elementary school. While many great models of learning such as Constructivist and Montessori methods promote activity and experience over passive absorption of information, we are still lacking a solid framework to introduce these soft skills to students in a way that progress can be tracked AND that they are finally valued as much as academic knowledge.

Meanwhile the workforce is demanding them, universities are struggling to develop them, and K–12 is waiting to be asked to develop them.

The World Economic Forum puts collaboration and working with others at the top of their skill sets to thrive in the #FutureofWork.

HOW ARE WE PREPARING STUDENTS FOR THIS?

Disrupting the Game of School

I just knew it was going to be the best experience ever! I had wrapped up weeks of prep with a colleague, and we were eager and ready to launch a project with students in her eighth-grade history class. The project challenged students to figure out how various types of media could create a resource more engaging than their traditional textbook. (Seriously, it was the same US history textbook I had in the eighth grade!) As we divided the students into groups to tackle various events of the Revolutionary War, none of us would imagine that the students would, as a class, create a one-hundred-twenty-page, interactive book that included first-person writing, images, animations, in-character videos, and a quiz at the end of the book. Using Book Creator, the students crafted incredible stand-alone interactive books—including one about the winter at Valley Forge with a Lakers color theme—that we later combined to the point of being unable to export the 1.2GB file off an iPad onto Google Drive. With excitement we sat down with each group of students to debrief and reflect on the experience. When we asked who we thought was the most successful group how they had liked the project, they said in near unison, "We hated it!"

Shocked, my colleague and I asked the students to clarify, and their response is one of those moments in the back of my head that keeps the passion and fire burning bright. They said they wished they could have just written an essay, completed some worksheets, and crammed for a unit test. They had perfected a strategy that took minimal effort on their part and didn't like having to improvise. In short, these students had mastered the game of school, and we were disrupting their game.

It is absolutely critical for us to disrupt the "Game of School" for our students. They need moments (the more frequent the better) to step outside of learning that is about the grades. We need to show our students that sometimes you put effort and energy into something because of the impact it makes and the people who can gain from your hard work.

After the media project was completed, one student asked if it would be the textbook for next year's eighth graders. That was a pivotal moment for my colleague and me because it gave us a moment to see the students taking pride in their work. We definitely wanted it to be an annual project, so the next step was to find out how our students could publish the content for an audience. With the help of the principal, we identified a few areas where fifth grade and eighth grade overlap. The end result was a second project focusing on the Bill of Rights in which students created a video in any style they wanted on one of the ten amendments. With audience understanding and experience in mind, our eighth-grade students gifted the videos to the lower grades, who were thrilled to learn from their upperclassmen.

Collaboration!

Celebrate Skills

One great way to promote collaboration is for students to celebrate their skills and abilities. Have the students survey each other around specific skills needed to make projects more valuable. In past classes, I have surveyed students to find out what production skills they have, whether it is in art, design, music, programming, or even acting. Giving those students the space to shine and improve the quality of group work is a great way to take a classic cooperative group project into the realm of collaboration.

Lead by Example

Leading by example is a great way to show the importance of collaboration in the classroom. By collaborating with your colleagues and creating interdisciplinary learning opportunities, you show your students what collaboration looks like and how it can possibly impact others.

Action Plan

The action plan is a great way to ensure that project goals are met and completed with all members involved. By assigning and making each team member accountable, it removes the greatest obstacle to group work—free riding.

Use Real World Problems

Students want to see their work and learning matter. By giving them real world examples to apply their learning, they are more eager to engage with projects and collaborate with others.

CHAPTER 5

IDEAS SHOULD LEAD TO ACTION

Chanoch l'naar al pi darko.
Teach the youth according to their way.
—(Mishlei 22:6)

Every child is an artist.
The problem is how to remain an artist once he grows up.
—Pablo Picasso

Kabbalah has an interesting way of looking at the Hebrew word for wisdom, חכמה (Chochmah). By breaking apart the letters of the word, it can be rearranged into a novel and powerful statement of what the essence of wisdom is. Wisdom can be defined as the summary of a person's experience, knowledge, and good judgment. While that definition is indeed accurate, it is a passive one. Wisdom in an active form is characterized by the continual search for lightbulb moments, those seeds of creativity that impact the world around you. The Kabbalistic approach is to break the word in half, re-arrange the letters and form two new words that give a whole new meaning to the word *wisdom*. (Hebrew is read right to left.)

WISDOM IS THE POWER OF *WHAT*. IT'S THE POWER OF LOOKING AT THE WORLD DIFFERENTLY AND THE POWER TO NOTICE THINGS THAT GO UNNOTICED BY OTHERS.

Wisdom is the power of *what*. It's the power of looking at the world differently and the power to notice things that go unnoticed by others. The true power of wisdom is not just asking why, but also asking what. What can be done? *What* can be done differently? What if we do this? What if we do that? If we begin these *what conversations* early on and continue to build on them as we get older, we can harness that power to do something great in the world.

One of the greatest adversaries of creativity is the idea that it starts with a single flash of inspiration or completely original thoughts. This fallacy stunts the growth of creativity or keeps it dormant altogether. It is entirely possible to be creative using existing ideas. Ideas, similar to seeds, contain the potential for even bigger ideas. You might not have created the seed, but you have the power to water it, nurture it, and help it grow into something utterly unique and exceptional. The water comes from our inspiration. Water is life, and we need to connect to creative people, especially outside of our industry, to think outside the box and give our creativity the extra minerals it needs. The challenge then becomes how to synthesize, remix, and mashup these ideas into something meaningful, something awesome, and something that is you.

In Chassidus, a school of Jewish mysticism, wisdom is considered an essential point, a flash, or a seed that contains that potential. The struggle is not just how to act on those lightbulb moments but how to notice them. Too often we doubt our own insights and end up latching onto ideas that are safe and convenient. Like the 30 Circle Challenge found in the toolkit at the end of the book, we have to consider both the potential quality and quantity of ideas. So where do we start? How do we take the knowledge and skills we have and do something about those lightbulb moments? You start planting. The hardest part about developing creative confidence is to stop expecting instant or near instant results. In today's world of Instagram, insta-coffee, and insta-outcomes,

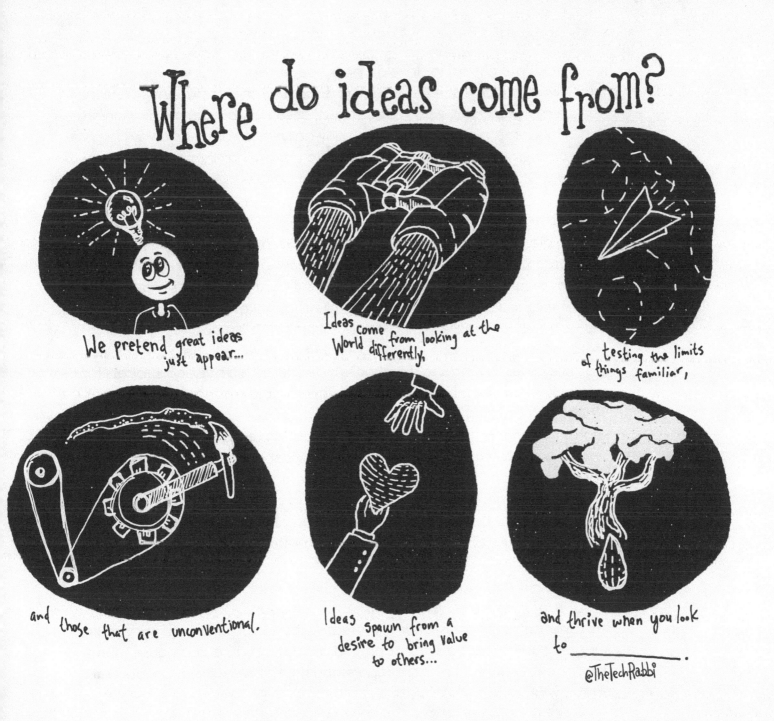

it is difficult but critical to develop patience. As educators we know it takes time—weeks, months, even an entire school year—for students to master certain concepts and skills. We must treat creative confidence and innovation in the same way! While we can't dilly dally, there are many ways to give students the time and space they need to act on their lightbulb moments.

Sketchnoting

If a picture is worth a thousand words, then sketchnoting is worth ten thousand! Sketchnoting is the process of creating a visual story from content you have consumed. This could be content from a lecture, song, book, or any other medium you encounter. While many sketchnote veterans have the capacity to create during a live talk, this isn't an easy entry point into sketchnoting. The reason why one of my favorite ways to help get students' creative juices flowing is to sketchnote is because it's a personal process that challenges the sketchnoter to create glyphs or icons that have meaning. What I love about sketchnoting is that it isn't about painting the next *Mona Lisa* or becoming the next Picasso. It's about developing a way of thinking and seeing the world that empowers you to connect symbols and words to big ideas. It is an incredible way to bolster visual communication skills while, at the same time, creating a great artifact to study from and teach others.

By looking at basic shapes, lines, and hieroglyphic markings, we can start to see how to build a big idea into a step-by-step experience to learn from.

Subsec 1—Basic Shapes

One of the coolest realizations in the 2D and 3D spaces of creativity is that the entire world is basically created by combining and subtracting squares and circles. So if you "can't" draw a stick figure or a house then try it right now. Draw your own stick figure and house below mine. Collaboration for the win!

Letters

ABCDEFGHIJK

abcdefghi

Frames

ABCDEFG

abcdefghij

ABCDEGHI

abcdefghijklmnop

Objects

@thetechrabbi

#Sketch50

Subsec 2—Create a Path

Then look at flow and frameworks. How do you solve the challenge of organization with a step-by-step process beyond a linear or vertical list?

A web? [graphic]

A winding path? [graphic]

A staircase? [graphic]

Each one of those paths captures a big idea that takes us back to those ideas being seeds that contain potential.

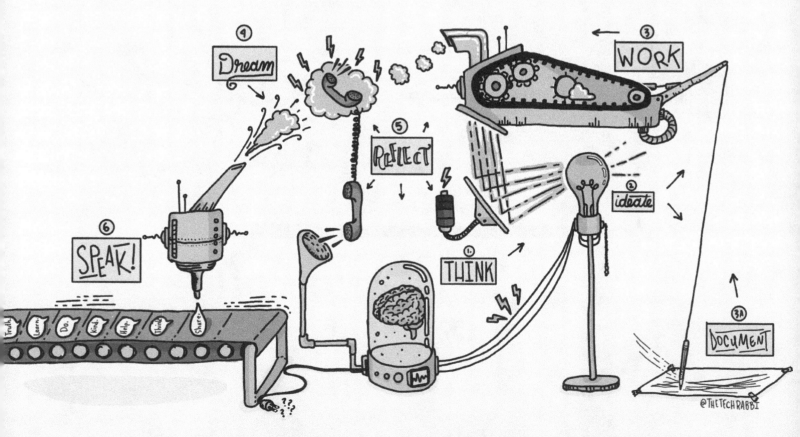

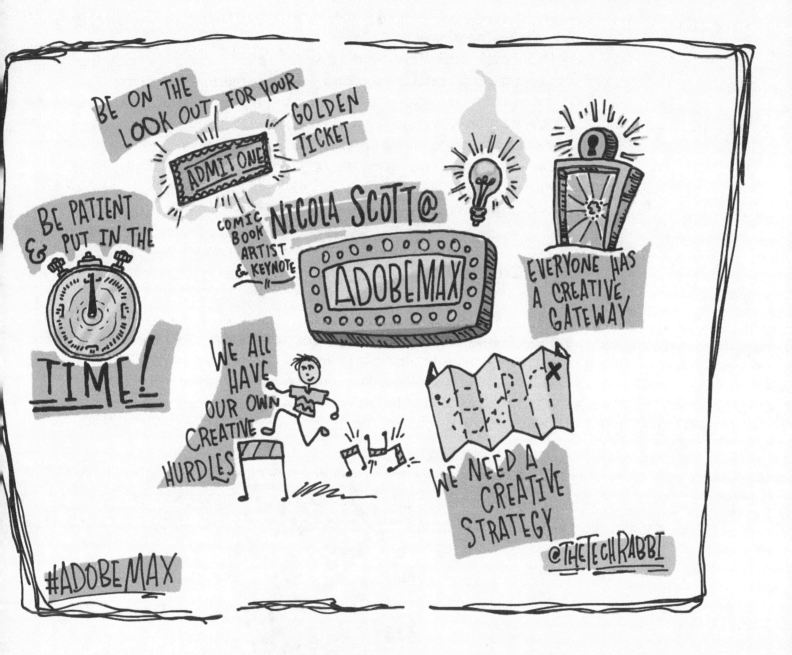

Subsec 3—The Power of Color

I will never forget *The Winter at Valley Forge* interactive book that featured a purple background and yellow text theme. The Lakers had not been in the championship for almost three years at this time, but the color was unshakable and distracting. Color Theory is a powerful way of connecting colors to ideas, emotions, and actions. Red could be love, murder, or danger. Yellow can be yield, happy, or fresh. This is another very tangible method of helping us bolster our creative capacity while gaining a skill that can strengthen our resumes.

Ideas Create Action

Sketchnote a TED Talk

Have students watch a TED Talk and sketchnote. Give them something they can watch, pause, and rewind. TED Talks are something powerful. The power lies in how the speaker constructs their story. Nancy Duarte has an incredible TED Talk on creating these types of stories, and nearly all of my keynote talks are modeled after this.

The gist is that stories that ebb and flow between *what is* and *what could be* resonate more with people. This approach reminds them of reality, gets them thinking, and with hope, offers them the opportunity to gain a new perspective around an idea. This makes them incredible to sketchnote because there is so much substance in a TED Talk in such a short period of time.

Sketchnoting is a great place to start because it gives us a concrete starting point for starting to apply our thinking in a completely new way. Providing ourselves with a framework and toolset to start expanding and documenting our thinking gives us a context to see how ideas can develop into something much greater once we act on them.

CHAPTER 6

TECHNOLOGY IS JUST A TOOL

In the 600th year of the sixth millennium, the gates of sublime wisdom will open and the wellsprings of lower wisdom will burst forth.
—The Zohar

People sometimes think technology just automatically gets better every year, but it actually doesn't. It only gets better if smart people work like crazy to make it better. That's how any technology actually gets better.
—Elon Musk

This quote from the Zohar has always fascinated me. The 600th year of the sixth millennium coincides with the year 1839, a year that represents the Industrial Revolution and many other incredible societal and technological advances and breakthroughs. It's more than that. The drive behind the industrial revolution of the 1700 and 1800s as well as the subsequent revolutions, including the fourth and current one driven by AI and other technologies, has always been about how technology can be a tool to provide incredible value to ourselves and others. When I was eight years old and lived in Southern California, my parents bought a video conferencing system for talking with my grandparents in Philadelphia. To this day, I could never figure out how my grandfather set it up on his end. The mammoth devices used a combination of wires to connect to our house phone and television, delivering a blurry 200x100 pixel image of my grandparents, whose movement was delayed by forty-five seconds as their voices echoed through the telephone. It was during one of those long conversations that I realized technology was the tool I was going to use to change the world. That is because, for me, having the latest and greatest tech was less about staying on the cutting edge and more about finding ways to make people's lives better.

Consider this riddle: I am a revolutionary device. I am lightweight, mobile, and fit easily into the palm of a person's hand. I have the capability to capture the world around me through shapes, words, and ideas. I can start conversations, connect people across the globe, help them collaborate, think critically, and share their creations. I am reliable, accessible, and effective. What am I?

A No. 2 Pencil. (Be honest—did I have you fooled?)

It is mission critical that we stop looking at technology as an experience in and of itself. The more we see it as a tool to help us accomplish tasks and goals, the more thoughtful its use can be as well as the

innovation that drives new technological advancements. There are plenty of tools, platforms, apps, and great devices out there, but none of them will help you succeed if you don't start with intent and purpose.

Technology is more than just a device. Technology is a solution to a problem that directly enhances or improves an experience or output. When we think about technology, we usually focus on smartphones, tablets, and even our classic Super Nintendo. Rarely do things like pencils, air conditioners, or a set of keys come to mind. We tend to view technology solely through the lens of electronically powered devices. A good history lesson would be to challenge students to explore how human communication evolved from cave paintings to Instagram posts.

Consumption and Creation

With the introduction of mobile technology, the opportunities for students to engage and interface with information quadrupled. Tablet technology, in particular, has created a new paradigm in which users can access, deconstruct, apply, and share knowledge in groundbreaking ways. For the most part, the evolution of technology has been a consumption-driven experience, and school has kept in with that approach. Today's technology and the social media revolution have shifted into an empowering and creator-driven experience. From YouTube to Instagram and the slew of software and hardware companies, there has been a new focus on helping creators create and ensuring that technology makes it simple and quick. The reality is that becoming a creator of content is easier and more accessible than ever before. The question that needs to be answered is why school hasn't valued this creator approach more beyond elective courses and outlier learning experiences.

To put this into context, you would need to have a near Star Trek level imagination as a media professional in the 1990s to believe an entire film could be scripted, planned, shot, edited, and produced all from a single device, let alone this monumental task be achieved by a six year old. That scenario—all too common these days—is proof that we are living in unbelievable times.

In school, we saw an oversaturation of niche consumption-based apps. These apps aspired to engage students through media and interactive experiences that still emphasized direct instructional practice and did little to challenge students outside of the memorized status quo. The flaw with these apps is they continue with the lower common denominator of learning and, even worse, are, in a way, more limiting than the textbooks they tried to replace. Not to mention the "digitized" textbook trend, now you had apps that were used for one unit and then discarded. In 2014, educational app development had a major growth spurt where you saw apps like Explain Everything and Book Creator take a new approach to how apps could be used. These apps joined the ranks of established Apple apps like iMovie and Keynote.

Today the opportunity for a complete shift in technology's role in student learning exists that can emphasize creation over consumption, or at the very least, the consumption is of peer-created work. It is in this area of creation-based technology integration that all efforts must be focused. This is the future of not just twenty-first-century learning but twenty-second-century learning and beyond.

Active and Passive Technology

As a piece of technology, a lead pencil is simple yet effective. But such devices are being overtaken by emerging technologies because they are what I call "passive technology." Passive technology tends to

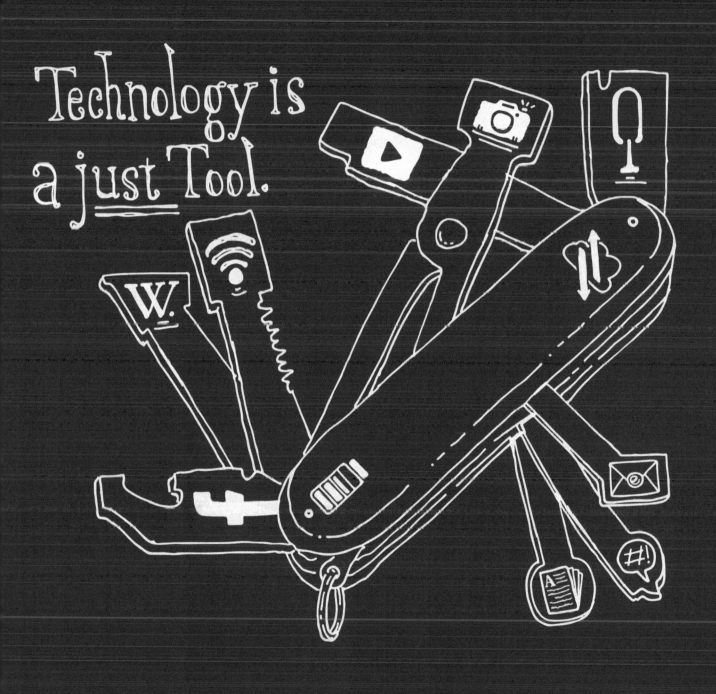

have a singular function, and it generally can be used in only one way. As technology continues to evolve, we find ourselves interfacing more and more with "active technology," technology tools that are multifaceted and multifunctional. These devices are mobile, agile, and efficient, allowing users to explore and redefine the boundaries of creativity, personal expression, and collaboration.

Active Output

Active technology allows users to participate in, rather than be passive recipients of, the experience. Without active technology, classrooms are severely limited in how they access, gather, apply, and share information. But with these tools, classrooms and individual learners can produce all kinds of active output—audio, visual, and hands-on interactive experiences—that can be put to excellent use as learning resources.

Audio

When we think about inclusivity in education, think about how far technology can take us. The use of audio recordings in the classroom does more than just include students with disabilities, which in and of itself is a massive accomplishment, but it includes a type of learner that might need to hear things twice but can't pause and rewind the teacher. Audio feeds into our social nature in a powerful way that promotes communication, dialogue, and the ability to archive learning in a new way. While audio isn't a new technology, we have seen significant advances of classroom application in addition to traditional voice recorders that can record a lecture. Audio becomes something that can be part of a student's project to infer understanding, where he or she might lack the capability of doing the same in written form. Simply put, audio has the ability to engage and involve so many more learners who might be lost in the shuffle in an overcrowded classroom.

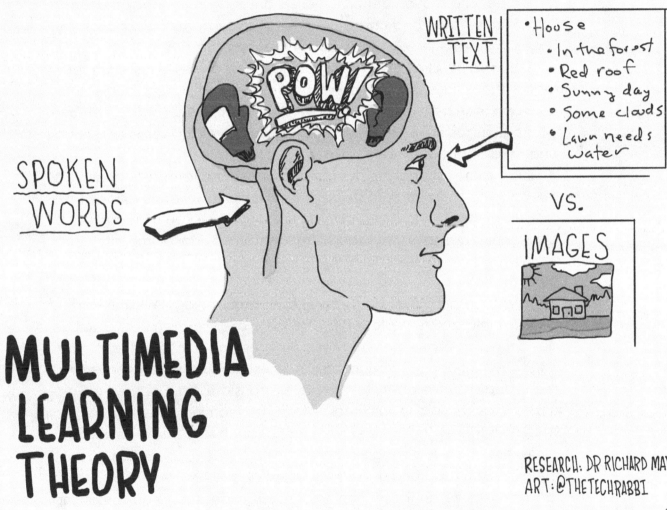

Visual

I think in pictures. Anytime I survey a group, a majority of them consider themselves to be visual learners, or visuals help them relate to and remember information better. If there is anything in this book that I can back with serious research, it's the area of visual communication. If you haven't heard of or read the work on multimedia learning theory by Dr. Richard Mayer, I strongly suggest you do. His decades of research show that, without question, your bullet point slide decks during your lectures do worse than nothing; they actually block listeners' ability to internalize information, as the brain competes between verbal words and visual ones and all but overloads.

Even more, visuals like photos and videos have an uncanny way of engaging users and creating a memorable experience. Look at the success of the film industry and think about how this could be applied to classroom learning without sacrificing academic rigor or integrity.

Kinesthetic

This is one of my favorite parts of tablet technology. While it started with the interactive whiteboard, the idea of giving learners a tactile device, which allows them to physically interface with it via their hands, is truly revolutionary. Through various kinesthetic engagements, tablet technology has the ability to completely transform how learners collaborate, explore, and create most awesome learning experiences. See what I did there? The mere existence of a touch-responsive device promotes the ability to engage in learning with a clear connection back to the critical mindset and skill sets discussed above. This type of back and forth is a requirement if technology's role is expected to be something that enhances or transforms classroom learning.

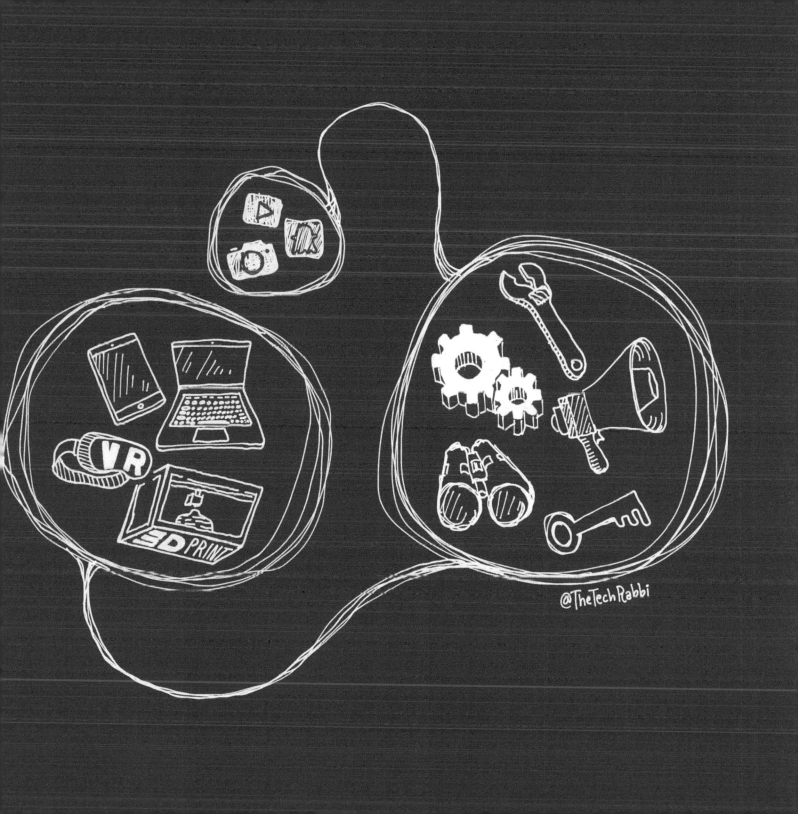

A Technology-Rich Environment

Educators often tout the benefits of building a technology-rich environment, but it's important to remember that quantity doesn't necessarily dictate quality. In fact, when using technology thoughtfully and intentionally, that use does not have to be constant. In many cases, the constant use of technology will not lead to increased engagement. For any teacher aspiring to build a tech-rich classroom, the key questions about use should be *why* and *how*, not *how often*. *Is the experience collaborative? Are students engaged in a self-paced experience? Are they creating something to call their own?* The true richness of technology's role in a classroom is how it allows students to learn and express themselves in new ways.

In education today, the embracement and use of technology many times simply replaces a tool to perpetuate an antiquated process that, while addressing efficiency, fails to provide students with a richer and more meaningful experience. From pen and paper to laptop for essay writing or the "Paperless classroom" that simply digitizes worksheets, we as educators are missing out on an incredible opportunity to empower our students to be creators with technology. Educators need training that brings awareness to what new opportunities are possible in the classroom because of technology. Until then we are not just putting the cart before the horse with technology use; we are strapping rockets and roller skates to the poor horse to make the cart move faster and promote "twenty-first-century learning."

For technology to truly serve students, educators must look at how much of the business world innovates. In that realm, innovation is communal and collaborative. And in a truly innovative learning space, students are allowed to break out of their silos, hone their skills and interests, and work together toward common goals. They are allowed to pursue knowledge at will, instead of waiting for a gatekeeper to dole out

20TH CENTURY TENDENCIES with 21ST CENTURY TOOLS

facts and figures according to some arbitrary schedule. In an innovative learning space, students achieve mastery of fundamental skills and knowledge, but that progress doesn't come at the expense of creativity.

The End of Keyboarding

Say goodbye to cursive writing and tell the keyboards their days are numbered. While schools are investing thousands of hours and dollars on developing strong keyboarding programs, top technology companies like Apple, Google, and Amazon are investing hundreds of thousands of dollars, if not millions, on ways to make keyboarding obsolete. Imagine dictating this entire 246 page book by mouth. While that might not seem enjoyable at the moment, five years from now, it might just be the norm.

Digitizing Twentieth-Century Learning

From the typewriter to the television to the desktop computer, generations have been presented with different tools destined to revolutionize education. Yet what headlines have we seen over the past few decades? See if you can find the common theme:

- "TV Replacing Teachers in the Classroom" *New York Times,* 1991,
- "Can Computers Replace Teachers?" *Time Magazine,* 2012
- "Will Computers Ever Replace Teachers? *The New Yorker,* 2014

More than twenty years later and headlines are still asking if technology's role in education is to replace educators. Facepalm.

One reason for this persistent worry is the sheer obsolescence of the education model we use in this country. Our schools and classrooms are trapped in a time warp, forced to operate within a one-hundred-year-old system that views students as indexable by age and delivers one-size-fits-all learning experiences in factory-style shifts. It's no wonder that

"Future Devices"

some innovators have used technology to focus on increasing productivity and cutting costs. But that's such a small part of what it can do. Technology holds the power to completely redefine our traditional learning experiences—much like it has already transformed and enriched our personal communication.

TECHNOLOGY MUST BE VIEWED AS A CATALYST FOR MATERIALIZING OUR IMAGINATION RATHER THAN A METHOD TO DIGITIZE THE STATUS QUO.

The Paperless Revolution

Going paperless is incredible, inspiring, and valiant even, but what's the purpose? Are we putting trees before our own children? I'm not taking a stance as much as I am starting a conversation. We need to be more thoughtful about how and why we validate certain practices in education because they impact our kids.

While digital is definitely the way for many experiences, I love the physical feel of a book and will always choose a book over a digital medium when looking to read something intellectually deep. Still, we print like crazy. I would guess that by first grade, the average student has amassed a hefty stack of completed worksheets. Ultimately, educators must recognize that digitizing twentieth-century learning experiences such as note taking and book reports can create new challenges for some learners, and we must work hard to put people before process.

Technology Integration Models

Frameworks and models are great because they give us perspective and a reference point for assessing our success and areas of growth. What's bad about models is they can pigeonhole you and leave you feeling unsuccessful or stuck. When I first saw allegorical infographics on the SAMR model, I must admit I was frustrated. One compared SAMR to coffee, which is such a subjective drink. For some, the Frapa-rapa-chapa-chino redefined coffee, but did it make it better? Was it necessary? For me, nothing is better than a cup of carefully crafted, black coffee. One thing the SAMR does well is remind us that redefining learning isn't appropriate or necessary for every activity, that it isn't an everyday occurrence. The SAMR can also help educators discern when it might be best to use no technology at all. When analyzing Dr. Ruben Puentedura's SAMR Model, substitution translates into no direct enhancement of the experience, but that can be counterproductive. A more thoughtful application of substitution, one that can increase engagement and even lead to augmentation of an experience, could be using a game-based platform that promotes visual connection to information through photos or video. In the end, technology should be a lens we use to examine the ways we are allowing students to engage with information.

The Next Ten Years

If I were to write a book about iPads and Chromebooks, it might well be obsolete within three to five years. It's not that the technology would disappear, but its role and relevance in education may change drastically. I want to focus on those technological processes that have mushroomed to epic proportions. They are the evergreen and ever-evolving processes that reside in the fields of computer programing, multimedia production, and storytelling. Through these lenses, I will share real, relevant, and reimagined ways to use technology to spark curiosity and allow students to experience learning in a meaningful way.

Coding Your Story

Computer code is a timeless technology that has evolved over time and still shows no indication of stopping—especially given that all technology runs on some sort of computer language. Today Python has become the main ingredient in many of the coding programs sweeping the nation. It provides the building blocks that are used to teach young minds powerful skills in the areas of critical thinking and problem solving.

As a technology aficionado, I love coding. There is something about building a string of code and watching the process unfurl that I find exciting and challenging. From HTML to Visual Basic, I enjoyed coding starting in high school and always kept it as part of my arsenal of odd skills. In 2013, when the *Hour of Code* launched, bringing simplified coding into the classroom, I asked myself, *What percentage of students will find coding to be a serious hobby, or even more, a future profession?* Without data to back it up, I predicted no more than five percent. What about the remaining ninety-five percent? What role can coding play in their learning? Many pro-coding educators will tout its ability to foster twenty-first-century skills such as higher-order thinking, problem solving, organization, and sequencing. While this might be true, what is the expense of using coding as the medium to acquire these skills? Is there another medium? Is coding the best choice?

For me, coding is a powerful and practical tool because at its root, coding is nothing more than telling a story with a plot, characters, dramatic structure, and most importantly, a sequential flow. When any of these elements are missing, it's hard to engage your audience. It is through storytelling that I have experienced some of my greatest technology integration moments, and I want coding to be no different

As twenty-first-century educators, we must embrace technology as a tool that empowers our students not only to share their ideas but to also believe those ideas can make a difference. We must emphasize twenty-first-century competencies because they give our students the ability to lead, articulate, solve, and redesign. It's not enough to simply memorize information and pass a test. The future requires something more of us, and whether it's programming the next groundbreaking application or better understanding project management, coding deserves a place in our classrooms. I challenge you to jump into coding, not because you need to develop the next new app, but because your story deserves to be shared.

Visual Impact Through Photo and Film

If a picture is worth a thousand words, imagine how many words could be conjured by sixty frames per second! One thing I realized early on in life is that I think in pictures. Needless to say, I was quite surprised when I first heard that others thought with words. Then I realized even thoughts made up of words are pictures as well. We are visual creatures. Still, in the classroom we rely mostly on verbal communication backed by technology in the form of text-based slideshows and words written on a board. This twentieth-century approach is not only outdated but leaving behind a majority of learners to struggle on their own to internalize information. It was developed with technologies available in the 1900s, primarily printed books, pencils, and paper. Today's educators can no longer ignore multimedia technologies when looking to support all learners in the classroom. When exploring how to integrate more multimedia and visual communication in your classroom, consider these three methods:

What do you think of when you see this photo? Now what about in the context of education's relationship with technology? Based on

Dr. Richard Mayer's work in multimedia learning theory over the past three decades, this image should create a visual marker for the conversation around it. This image then cannot just connect "visual learners" but create a memory marker for all learners when trying to remember information that was presented. This, more than a list of bullet points or even a sentence or two, will create a memorable moment for learners.

So then what would happen if you were to build a lecture or conversation around a slide deck with *no* words?

When someone learns, the more senses that are activated, the more memorable the learning can be. Challenge students to create artifacts of learning that contain visual, audial, and kinesthetic elements. When comparing a worksheet or essay to a multi-touch book containing audio files, video, and photos, all the while promoting touch and movement, ask yourself which experience is more memorable. This makes the idea of giving students a challenge of using multimedia to assess their own knowledge while allowing their work to be used for others to learn from borderline transformational.

If you ask most students, they live a double life. One in school and one out. As educators we must question why this is the case. We need to bridge the gap by using the platforms they use every day to create content and engage with their friends. This doesn't mean that Snapchat needs to come into the second grade classroom, but it does mean that we need to learn a thing or two from the world of marketing, advertising, and social media. We need to understand the power of visuals to not just influence but engrain a message into the minds of those who interact with it. This can be done in any classroom with any content. Multimedia allows us to explore ways for students to capture the theme of learning with a strong visual and a quote. Challenge students to use multimedia to be clear, concise, and of course, memorable.

It's Your Story So Tell It!

Growing up, I hated writing, and here I am publishing a book. Where was the disconnect? As an educator, I have discovered that it all boils down to one single word—*essay*. I don't think there's anything fun about essays. The good news is, based on the results of a recent Google search, it looks like essays are on the decline.

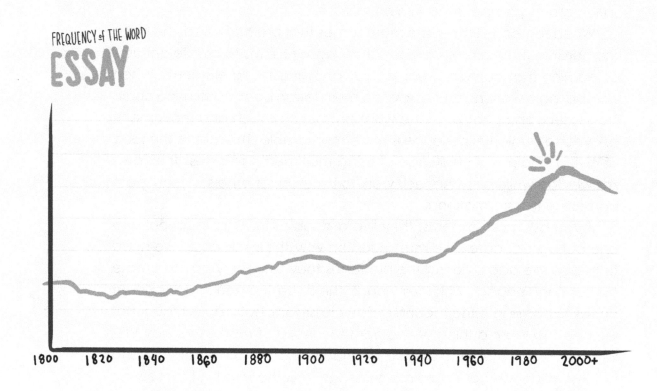

FREQUENCY of THE WORD
ESSAY

1800 1820 1840 1860 1880 1900 1920 1940 1960 1980 2000+

It's not that the essay in and of itself is bad; it's just that the essay has always been framed with a focus on *how* to write rather than *why* on earth you would want to engage in such an activity. Storytelling, on the

STORYTELLING IS THE FUTURE!

other hand, takes writing and gives it life. We love to tell stories and we love to hear them. Stories have a soul. They entice us, teach us, and challenge us to use our imaginations. With this in mind, try challenging your learners to write from their passions and not for the process. And give them a little freedom! Allow your students to write with the instrument of their choice—pencil, pen, keyboard, or even voice—to tell their stories. I predict that this freedom will infuse a new energy and meaning into topic sentences, paragraphs, and transitions.

In addition, challenge your learners to explore a wide range of writing, including comic books, novels, instruction manuals, magazines, fliers, and blogs. The written word is all around! This approach might sound a bit excessive or over the top, but that's what needs to happen in today's classroom because that's what is happening in the other parts of their lives.

Storytelling is the future! Don't believe me? Look no further than social media. Its essence is sharing, and Instagram, Twitter, Snapchat, and Facebook are all embracing storytelling through photo and video. This isn't a fad. Storytelling goes back thousands of years, and it's woven into the way we live our lives. But the tools are new and different, and we must bring them into our classrooms to keep the core components of education relevant and engaging. This is how we will develop the next generation of readers and writers.

Why We Must Look at Wisdom, Understanding, and Knowledge Differently in the Digital Age

The dictionary definitions of the three terms provide interesting insight.

wis·dom

/ˈwizdəm/ ◀))

noun

the quality of having experience, knowledge, and good judgment; the quality of being wise.

un·der·stand·ing

/ˌəndərˈstandiNG/ ◀))

noun

1. the ability to understand something; comprehension.

knowl·edge

/ˈnäləj/ ◀))

noun

1. facts, information, and skills acquired by a person through experience or education; the theoretical or practical understanding of a subject.

How many times do we confuse knowledge with understanding? How many times do we equate having knowledge with wisdom? The truth is that the three words are light years apart and my observation, as a student, teacher, and administrator, is that, in education today, many consider knowledge as the highest quality output for students. I'm not trying to devalue knowledge. It is important to know things. The problem with knowledge is that a robot can have knowledge. It can have under-standing as well. What a robot will lack is true wisdom, as such a quality has so many layers beyond information and synthesis. With that in mind I propose, the following question:

Which is more valuable? The ability to know everything or the ability to find anything?

The ability to research, compile, and curate information is more about processing information than memorizing it. To knowledge's credit, you need to have a foundational level of knowledge to succeed in most tasks, but if you know how to search for information and actually use it, then I would say you have advanced further than the student who memorized information for a worksheet that was turned in to his or her teacher.

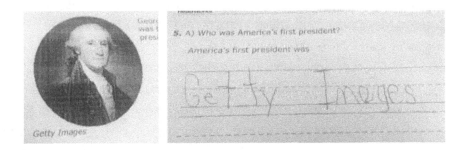

I first saw this image last week as part of the Twitter idea battle. As a designer, I am trained to seek out subtle details as I look to solve prob-lems. The meme's intent is to show that students who simply Google things without context or knowledge will fall prey to an ultimate level of idiocy and confuse an image source with the information they should be looking for. Now I, for one, believe that this image is doctored. Why? Besides the three to four visual markers in how the content is placed, what stands out the most is that the original image doesn't come up in a Google search. Imagine that. A student as young as six or seven, who can't spell images, or a teacher, looking for a worksheet image, runs a Google Search for this image and found an image of President Getty Images, yet I can't find it at all? I know Boolean strings for searching and how to do deep Google searches, yet the only images that come up are duplicate images of the original meme.

This stimulated a second question, which is why does the conduit to knowledge, i.e., facts and information acquired by someone, matter? If a robot, adult, or peer supplies you with knowledge, why does either have an edge on the other? This student example doesn't show a lack of knowledge; it shows a lack of understanding.

Since all experiences contain a trace of good, this Twitter interaction did inspire me to locate a few well-cited research articles on the topics of learning in the digital age.

While there is certainly research that concludes technology can and does prevent learning and stifles academic gains, these three sources, including one from MIT's very own lifelong kindergartener Mitchel Resnick, are definitely food for thought in this discussion of the what, why, and when of knowledge. For one, Dr. Resnick clearly challenges the notion of continuing that "while new digital technologies make a learning revolution possible, they certainly do not guarantee it. In most places where new technologies are being used in education today, the technologies are used simply to reinforce outmoded approaches to learning."

If the embracement and advancement of technology in other industries is not enough, he also uses his article as a platform to question people's correlation between education, learning, and "information." The value that teachers bring is in how they nurture complex reasoning and problem solving. I personally find it degrading of the teaching profession that they are mere databases that distribute information.

I strongly believe that education today is still struggling with how to restructure and redesign learning experiences around technology's role in both input and output of knowledge, understanding, and wisdom. I also believe that much of the educational research conducted around technology's role in teaching and learning fails (unlike these sources) to critique how antiquated educational processes still produce mediocre results, even when technology is incorporated into the process. All other industries use technology to advance, shift, develop, and change, while education is using it to validate and perpetuate a century-old model of factory-style learning experiences.

Creative Exploration with Technology

How To Create Epic Diagrams with Adobe Spark Post

While there are no shortage of awesome and very out-of-the-box ways to use Adobe Spark products, it is important to note that simple and routine tasks can be completely transformed using the platform.

Take this fill-in-the-blank diagram worksheet, for example:

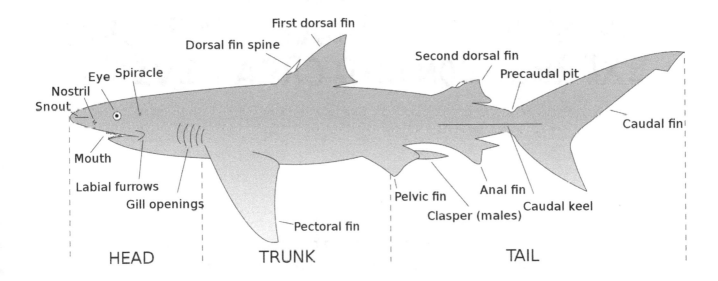

Worksheets such as these are rarely engaging for students, and the product output results in twenty to thirty replicas turned in to the teacher. They lack personal connection and expression and do little to get students invested in creating high-quality work. A question I often get from teachers is, "Should content coverage be sacrificed to promote personal expression?" The answer is both yes and no. Should you sacrifice six to ten hours of coverage? I will leave that to your discretion as a teacher. What I will say is that,

EVERY TEACHER CAN SPARE TWENTY MINUTES TO PROMOTE ENGAGEMENT THROUGH PERSONAL EXPRESSION AND CREATIVITY.

By using Adobe Spark Post, you can have students creating that same evidence of learning, with a personal flare that promotes visual communication and problem solving skills beyond mere memorization.

The project is simple and can be completed quickly as a summative assessment piece. As you see in my video demo, I even used some of the time toggling between colors and fonts to find something that popped but was thematically appropriate.

Note: Hot pink and yellow **POP!** The challenge will be how it is defended as a good color scheme for sharks. The answer is that if you want the color to aid in making it memorable, then yes, you should use crazy colors!

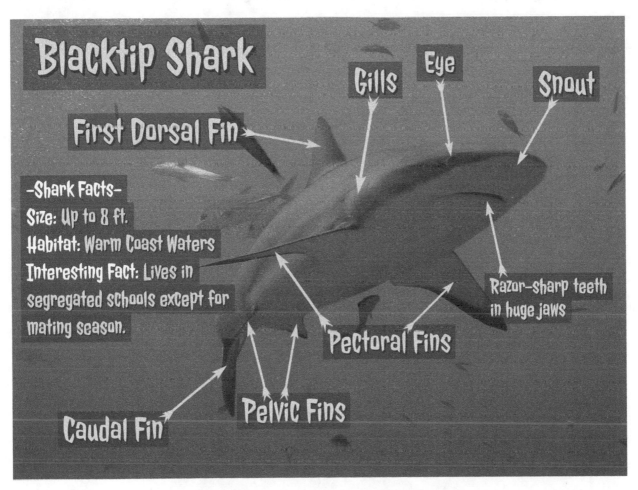

Step 1:   Research your topic so you are prepared with your notes and knowledge.

Step 2:   Start your project size by selecting Start From Scratch > Select A Size > Standard > Slide (4:3) > Next.

Step 3:   Search for a dynamic photo that represents your topic in an interesting way. Consider how traditional diagrams typically use an image that is a side view or cross section. Can you find a photo of your object in an interesting composition?

Step 4: Choose a text box style. Once set, duplicate it for each label. (Note: Consider how the background color of the textbook, opacity, and line spacing improve your design.)

Step 5:   Choose an icon that can point. Once set, duplicate it for each label. (Note: Be creative but thoughtful. An arrow in the example is a good choice, but maybe there is a shark icon that can work as well.)

Step 6:   Adjust the composition by rotating the icons (arrows) and positioning the text boxes (labels) into their correct places.

Step 7:   Save your image on your device and share it with your teacher.

Optional, But Awesome, Step 8: Upload your design to a shared Google Slides project to be used as a study guide, classroom discussion piece, or class portfolio project.

CHAPTER 7

DON'T WAIT FOR PERMISSION

The world says that if you cannot crawl under an obstacle, try to leap over it. However, I say, leap over it in the first place! *l'chatchila ariber!*"
—Rabbi Shmuel of Lubavitch

Le mieux est l'ennemi du bien.
(The perfect is the enemy of the good.)
—Voltaire

I waited twenty years for someone to say, "Take your art, and do something amazing with it." I didn't hear those words in kindergarten, or in high school, or even from my first college art professor. It wasn't until I had graduated with a degree in printmaking that a professor told me that. In a way, it felt like he was finally giving me permission to fly free and forge my own path. I wonder how often that happens. How often do we wait for permission—not because we're doing something wrong but because we're doing something beyond? Venturing into the unknown is scary. With creativity, that fear is multiplied by ten. But we must persevere on our own and not wait for experts or authority figures to encourage us and give us permission to go above and beyond, outside the box, or to a place where there are no more boxes. We must grant ourselves permission. As the old Yiddish saying goes, "'A Shailah Macht Treif' (A question makes it automatically not Kosher)."

This chapter is written for every person who has spent any amount of time holding back because they didn't have permission.

Redefining Good Work

School has conditioned us to believe that perfection is the aim and that life is a summative game. A perfect score, whether it's an A+, a 4, or a 1600, is an indicator of our success, or lack thereof, for the first twelve to sixteen years of our lives. The traditional education model has also trained us to believe that if we cannot attain perfection, we are merely *average*. Meanwhile, out in the real world, the leading edges of technology, medicine, and commerce are built on the backs of repeated failure. As we discussed in Chapter 2, failure is a formative process, not a summative experience. If we can remember that and overcome this pervasive fear of failure, we will achieve an even deeper understanding of resilience and risk taking, and finally debunk the myth that our work must be perfect.

LIFE IS GRADED ON THE CURVE

Now.

This isn't a pass to be careless, disorganized, or irrational. The creative process I am pitching in this book is not an excuse to settle for mediocrity and produce flawed work. Just keep in mind that life is graded on a curve, and at some point, you have to get your hands dirty and start doing. If you're lucky, someone will be there to help you as you refine your craft and hone your skills.

Take YouTubers, for example. Many people assume that individuals like Casey Neistat woke up one day, made some videos, and now have more than eight million subscribers, and not a single video with less than a million views.

False.

Most successful content creators produced between 200 and 500 videos before their content became notable or influential. My reason for sharing this isn't to inspire you to become the next YouTube star (but please do if you feel you have what it takes); it's to point out how many imperfect, even straight-up bad, videos have to be made before someone can consistently create high-quality content. We're not taught to think this way in school. Media creation is an elective, and all skills involved in turning a passion into a profession are soft. We can't even talk about producing imperfect work because that would result in a failed test, a poor grade, and the end of the world as we know it. Or can we?

Can we create small pockets of time for failure? Can we create moments where students learn about people who refined a product through experimentation and exploration? To satiate students' curiosity and empower them to do great things, we must. Our view of what constitutes good work must evolve. The world has changed, and the internet, social media, and power of your passion are changing the world. Technology shows us, on a daily basis, that there is no *complete* or *done;* there is only an *update.*

Strategies for Overcoming the Fear of Perfection

Sadly, there is no tried-and-true guidebook for teaching young people to resist the lure of perfection, redefine good work, and treat failure as an opportunity for growth. But I know it's possible because I've done it, and if I had to do it again, here are three strategies I would use:

Find a Mentor

If you ask successful people to list practices that helped them achieve success, I can almost guarantee one factor was a good mentor. Mentors are powerful because they are living proof of what is possible and can help you avoid classic mistakes while pushing you to move forward. For me, my mentors have been instrumental in my success. Whether a spiritual mentor, a professional one, or even a mentor to learn how to be the best father I can be, each one brings value to my life and helps me become stronger. So how do you find one? Some people might benefit from a distant mentor. My distant mentor is Tina Seelig. As of publishing this book, I have never met her, but I read her books, engage with her on social media, and have even had a chance to engage in conversation over email. Another mentor of mine is Rabbi Moshe Levin, whom I engage with and seek guidance from on a nearly daily basis. Other

mentors wish to remain anonymous and help me out of the goodness of their hearts. Wherever you find your mentor, make sure you find people who have their hearts in what they do and the desire to help others grow.

Build Your Brand

If you work with high school students, introduce them to LinkedIn. Help them understand how to build a professional network, connect with people in specific fields, and write a clear, concise bio that doesn't reek of buzzwords. By developing a professional online presence, students will become more aware of what true failure looks like and how to manage short-term setbacks.

Explore interesting experiences: At the high school where I work, my goal is to ensure that every student graduates having participated in at least one MOOC. Whether it's project management, winemaking, or intro to Python, the best way to become self-aware and understand what you're good at is to work hard at something where failure is highly likely. Taking a MOOC or another online course gives students the opportunity to grow and learn something they feel is valuable or interesting without the pressures of summative assessment.

Avoid Making Comparisons

On your creative journey, you will interact with all kinds of people. I see incredibly talented people succeeding, often in the same niche that my work falls into. They travel around the world, they're sought after, and they're always ranked in those top innovator articles. It's outright intimidating, and sometimes it can make you doubt yourself and what you have to offer. But those thoughts are lies, a harmful byproduct of the fallacy of perfection. Don't go comparing someone else's middle to your beginning. All that will do is prevent you from making your mark on the world.

WHEN YOU COMPARE YOUR BEGINNING TO SOMEONE ELSE'S MIDDLE, YOU MISS THE CHANCE TO CREATE YOUR OWN JOURNEY.

@THETECHRABBI

Passion as Profession

In 2018, I had the incredible opportunity to be one of the keynote speakers at the ISTE conference. I want to first preface that while I acknowledge my expertise and good work, this was, without question, a miracle from G-d. I believe that when you are honest, do good work, and desire to help people, G-d gets you where you need to be. What was trying to prevent that success was the voice inside my head still demanding perfection and saying that if I failed to deliver it, I would let down thousands of people.

Thinking creatively is full of challenges. There is no way around it. Whether it's a limit on resources and tools, or location, or even access to collaborators, there will always be some reason to postpone getting started. Consider the world of YouTube and its stars, influencers, and successful creators. When you look at creatives like Marques Brownlee, Peter McKinnon, and Sara Dietschy, you see three talented people with hundreds of thousands to millions of subscribers and views. In short, they do what they love and get paid for it.

Let's say you give the YouTube thing a try. After a dozen videos, you might start comparing yourself to other, more successful personalities. You focus on the opinions of others. You start to doubt your vision, your message, everything you have to say. *Why aren't people interested in my work? I must not be creative. I must not be talented. I must not be interesting.*

Wrong.

THINKING CREATIVELY IS FULL OF CHALLENGES

The reason I use YouTube creators as an example is that many people don't respect or take seriously the industry of content creation. If a sixth grader told you she wants to be a YouTuber and create videos around her passion for wildlife preservation or makeup, would you have your doubts? Take Mya for example, aka FullTimeKid , who creates what are in her words, "fun educational tricks, cute crafts, songs and surprises that kids and parents will enjoy" for her nearly 80,000 subscribers. She had a passion to create videos around her interests and, with a support parent, made it happen. Why can't school be a place to inspire and cultivate such passion?

I once read an article that a school actually banned students from putting that as their top choice for a career day event. Meanwhile, not only is it a billion-dollar industry, most other industries are looking at these creators to learn about storytelling, product reviews, how-to tutorials, and teaching. Yes, teaching. Most of the successful YouTubers, including those mentioned above, are educators. They don't realize it or might even deny it, but they are teaching millions of people about technology, media creation, and storytelling, and having fun while doing it. And their success is not only about views or stardom. It's also about value. They provide value because they are talented at researching, planning, actualizing, and refining their communication and literacy skills around their specific passions.

Now more than ever, students have the ability to do whatever they want with their lives. In the past, parents dreamed of their sons and daughters becoming doctors, lawyers, and astronauts. Thanks to the internet, anyone willing to put in the work can build a profession based on their passions, interests, and talents.

I want to emphasize that you must have exemplary communication skills—verbal, visual, and written—to succeed in the world of content creation. I once spoke with a friend who works in the world of advertising. I was telling him about this incredibly entertaining product ad that blew me away, and I realized I couldn't recall the name of the company or what it was selling. But it was an awesome video, and I had spent several minutes talking about it. My friend told me that is the difference between a creative ad and a creative video. You can have a great script, full of humor and irony, and still fail to effectively communicate your message to your audience. After mulling over his words, it struck me that our students are often assigned media content projects with the blanket encouragement of "Be creative!" As a result, the core message of their topic is lost in a sea of entertaining fluff.

IT IS CRITICAL THAT WE HELP OUR STUDENTS UNDERSTAND THE POWER OF GOOD COMMUNICATION AND STORYTELLING.

It is critical that we help our students understand the power of good communication and storytelling. That is memorable for an audience: another great anecdote for the power of being a strong educator, facilitator, and teacher. These creators thrive because the internet has provided them with a platform where a global audience comes to find value. You don't have to wait for a college degree, support from a network insider, or a solid resume. You just have to want to create something that provides value for others.

Don't Wait, Just Start Doing!

The reason I became an educator was to dispel the myth of perfection. I wanted to teach young people to reject the fallacy that anything short of perfection is average or even failure. That kind of approach to education is dangerous. It robs students of the opportunities to take risks and grow, telling them instead to wait for perfection.

If I waited for perfection, I could have missed out on:

- Blogging
- Sharing on social media
- Presenting at conferences
- Running workshops for educators
- Creating flexible learning spaces that aren't about high-priced furniture
- Developing programming around entrepreneurship that is hard to assess and turn into data but is life-changing for students
- Writing this book
- Connecting with my readers and building a community around creativity and design in education

So many opportunities for each and every one of us exist. All we have to do is start.

Prototype to Help You Start

Rapid Prototyping

Rapid prototyping is an awesome way to get started and to stop over-thinking and waiting for perfection. The process is simple and straightforward. You create teams of five and six and give them a set amount of time and materials to create a prototype that solves a problem.

The Homework Machine

I introduce students to rapid prototype through the homework machine. I give each group the following materials.

1. 1 sheet of cardboard
2. 10 straws
3. 1 roll of duct tape
4. 5 sharpies
5. 3 pieces of paper
6. 6 (safety) box cutters

I introduce them to the Shel Silverstein Poem "The Homework Machine" and challenge them to create their own Homework Machine in thirty minutes. After completing the challenge, in a sentence or two, the students then each have to share one of the functions of their machine. The activity always has the students fully engaged, imaginations raging, and it almost always becomes a teachable moment of just starting and not waiting to figure it out, perfect it, or come up with a professional product on the first shot.

CHAPTER 8

CREATIVITY IS A HANDS-ON EXPERIENCE

Creativity without failure is like being lifted to the top of a mountain without the climb. It may be fun, but it is not an achievement.
—Rabbi Lord Jonathan Sacks

The best way to predict the future is to create it.
—Alan Kay

When you look at past experiences where creativity flourished and memorable moments were created, how many worksheets were used? How many projects with a single, clearly defined outcome were required? Creativity cannot exist where rote and rigidity reign supreme, but it thrives when learning experiences are open-ended and designed to evoke a sense of curiosity and wonder. Within this kind of space, young people can engage in hands-on learning and develop skills and expertise that cannot be easily replaced by a machine or algorithm. They enjoy the freedom of the kinesthetic exertion that can bolster and hone our innate and sometimes hidden creativity.

The Key to Self-Awareness Is Experimentation

Self-awareness is all the rage right now. Most business and motivational gurus tout it as the linchpin to success, happiness, and everything in between. While they are on point, it is a shame that it takes someone ten to twenty years *after* school to discover that they a) have no self-awareness, b) are committed to a course of action contrary to what they love, and c) feel helpless and unable to solve this challenge. I was fortunate. My failures in high school left me without a golden ticket to a top college, and it was a huge advantage. The situation required me to get serious about what I was going to do in life. I was forced to figure out what I was good at to make a future for myself. The irony that I will never be able to shake is how I ended up pursuing a profession in education, an industry I really didn't care much for. What drives me, almost nine years into the journey, is an ongoing passion for helping students and teachers learn from my mistakes and discoveries.

Self-awareness starts with wonder—and at the age of six, not twenty-six! Think about that for a moment. "Where do you want to be in five years?" should not be a difficult question to answer. If you do not have

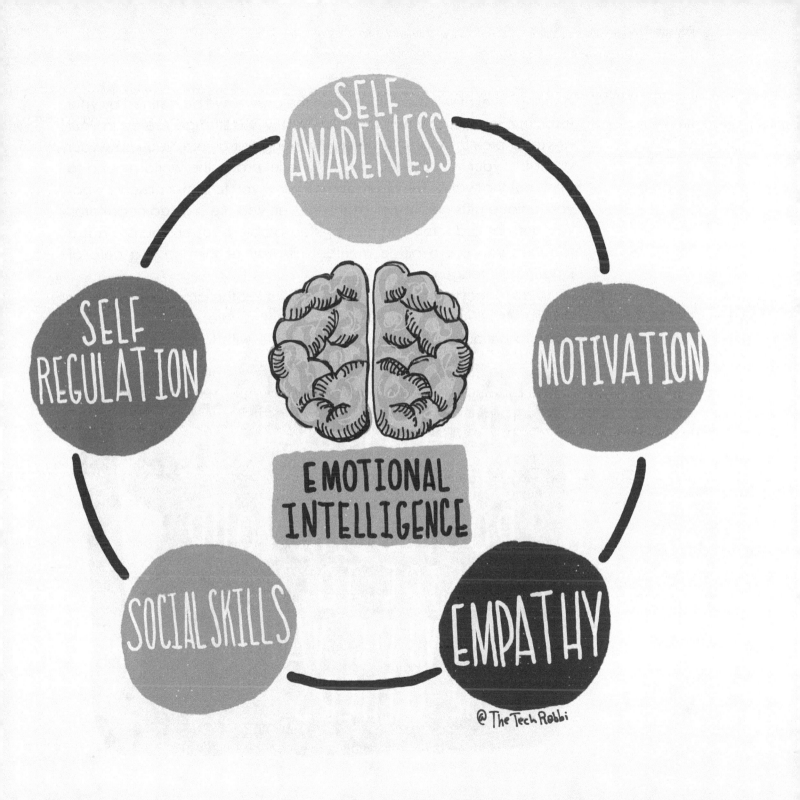

a strong level of self-awareness, then the answer will be defined by your job, your money, or your products. Creativity is strongly rooted in your desire to provide value for others. By being self-aware, you know your strengths, your weaknesses, and how to leverage the world around to bring out that value. This approach will allow you to better observe what your unique gifts are. You are not a lawyer; you are a gifted negotiator. You are not a doctor; you are a gifted problem solver. You are not a teacher; you are a gifted mentor. This way of thinking is a core of Emotional Intelligence (EQ).

In my entrepreneurial studio course, I think the greatest growth for students is self-awareness. By becoming self-aware, students are more open to critique and criticism, comfortable with failure, and open to

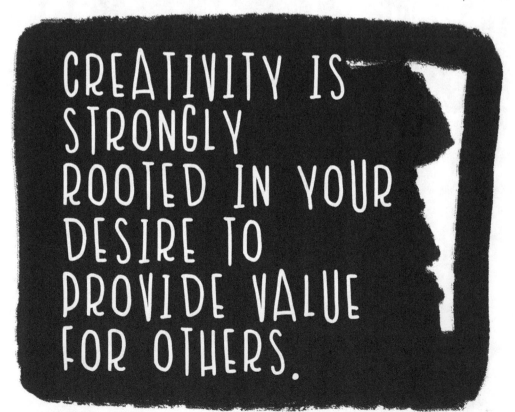

CREATIVITY IS STRONGLY ROOTED IN YOUR DESIRE TO PROVIDE VALUE FOR OTHERS.

reworking and refining their projects, allowing creative thinking to inject greatness into their work. Sure, I want a group of students to come up with the next Airbnb and scale their company, skip college, and make millions. That's nice, but that's not the litmus test for success. The measuring stick for me is how students' perspectives are changed and the confidence and alacrity that comes with the experimentation that happens during the year. That self-awareness is found in some of the most interesting experiences for students.

Let's take John and Alex for a second (not their real names). John and Alex have an idea. They are sophomores in high school and lean toward a more "Go get 'em" approach to life. They have an idea for an app and they promise me they have brainstormed and researched just like my script instructs. They're now at the point of prototyping, and they are more than excited, until one day, Rick walks in. In seconds he destroys their hopes and dreams by flipping open his phone and showing them their app idea, except it's not theirs; it's someone else's, and they have already taken their startup to scale, raking in over $50 million in venture capital. As I watched them pick up the shattered pieces of passion, I sat down with them to reflect on this process. "How did this happen? How did it take us so long to figure out the idea was already an app?" they asked me. I asked them if they researched, and they were adamant that they did. The truth is they did research, but their ability was limited to Googling "parking app." In thirty seconds, I was able to find the top ten parking-related startups through a database called Crunchbase, which gives me company information, including growth, funding, acquisitions, and team member information. Sure, self-awareness is rooted in how well you understand your passions, values, and morals. Those are very abstract states of being. A more concrete skill would be how well you research. If you don't understand the world around you, what resources exist, available opportunities, and emerging innovation, how can you nurture that self-awareness? If we were able to nurture students' self-awareness early on, then they would understand that the skills associated with research are incredibly valuable.

This takes a skill that, by many students, is perceived in a range from useless and boring to something only done in school. Meanwhile *Forbes* states the top reason startups fail is that there is "no market need." Doesn't that sound basic? Sure, running out of money, lacking the right team, and getting outcompeted are real business challenges. They aren't the top one, though. The top ranked reason is due to poor marketing research. That is a big deal.

Time to explore and develop self-awareness isn't in ninth grade. It's in kindergarten. Their success will allow the academic knowledge and skills of secondary education and beyond to make more sense. "What's the point of this?" isn't as much of a question on the topic or activity as it is in students' inability to incorporate that experience or knowledge in their lives. If it truly cannot be integrated, then we as educators better question the purpose and role of whatever it is that is being met with resistance. Math, history, and science make a whole lot more sense when you understand their long-term importance and application. If it is just something we need to learn because there is a test to get to the next stage of school, don't expect students to be soaking up your lecture and running to do more work in your class.

Let's get practical. Whether you are six, sixteen, or sixty, it is never too late to develop self-awareness. Here are three ideas to consider:

Experimental Experiences

Whatever you want to call it, 20-percent time, passion projects, or genius hour, students need to engage in unscripted open-ended experiences within the structured and mentor-supported space of school. I know there is little to no time, but you need to weigh the risk of your students not learning this or that against the value of learning to build their passion, perseverance, and problem-solving abilities. Imagine if the first two weeks of school were dedicated to a design-driven experience that focused on exploration, team building, and helping others? Imagine what the class dynamic would look like after that!

Reflection

Reflection is huge. It is a key characteristic of almost any successful person. Whether it's Steve Jobs, Elon Musk, Meg Whitman, or Sheryl Sandberg, reflection is an important part of their lives. When failure is no longer viewed as the enemy and risk is encouraged, students will be able to learn the art of reflection. In time it will become not just a reactive and reflexive process, but something that is proactive and intentional. In Judaism we have an interesting custom that many engage in. It is called a *Cheshbon Hanefesh,* which translates to an accounting of the soul. In observing this custom, you bookend your day with two questions, one posed in the morning and the other in the evening:

1. What good will I do today?
2. What good have I done today?

Reflection sounds simple, but in practice, it is really challenging to keep up. It allows you to think about who you are and what you are doing; what can be improved, what should be removed, and what could be introduced. For an educator, true reflection is certainly more difficult than filling out a worksheet or completing a scripted three-day activity. But it's also a lifelong skill that can enrich the lives of your students. It might not be this year or even before graduation, but when your third grader turns thirty-four, they might remember the opportunity you gave and the inspiring stories that fostered their creative thinking.

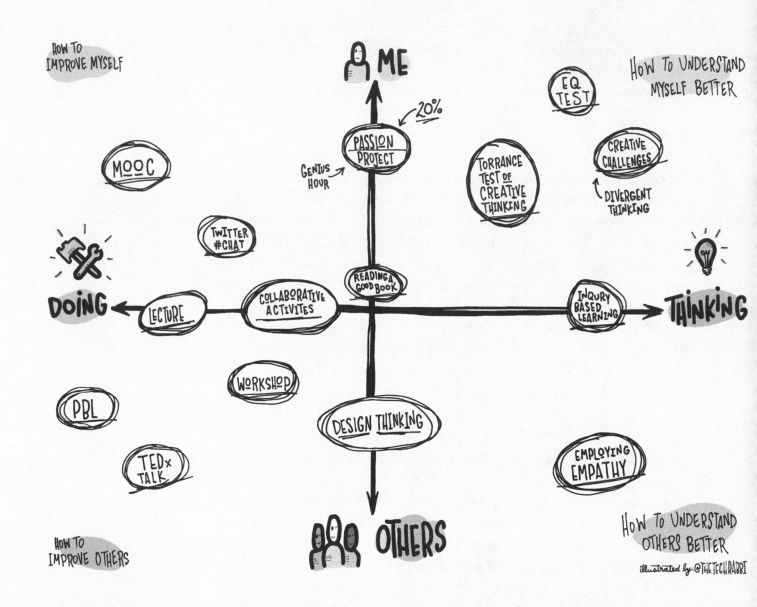

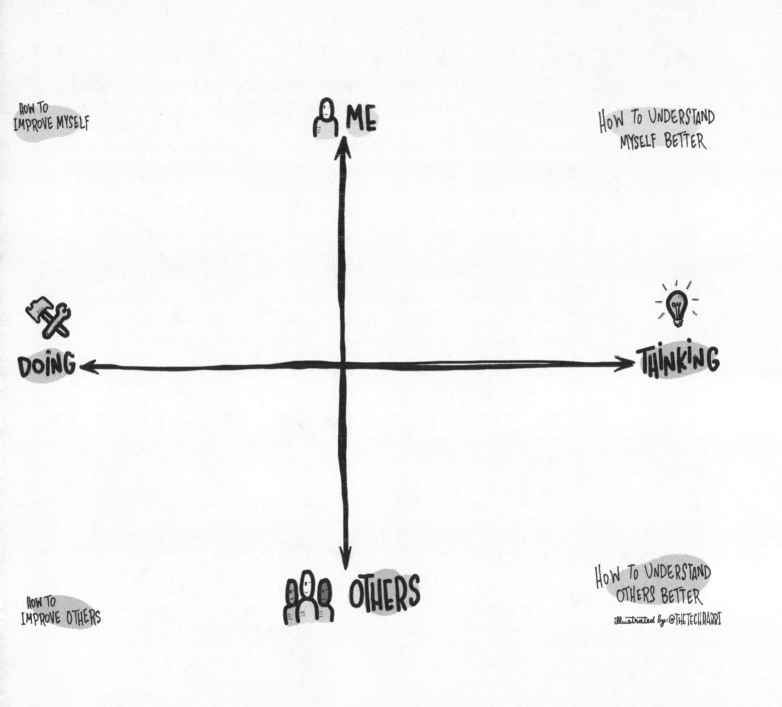

Students Teaching Students

Students learning through teaching others is not a new approach by any means. This pedagogical method has been part of classroom learning for centuries, maybe even millennia. With the advancement of technology and an emphasis on collaborative practice in the world of work, we have an incredible opportunity as educators to promote new methods of practice involving student facilitation of learning. There are multiple platforms that come into play, but the main drive has to be in how technology, publishing, and student learning can be a vehicle to provide benefit for others. This approach, for me, was inspired by Erin Olson, an educator from Iowa whom I connected with on Twitter and finally met face to face at an ISTE conference. This Tweet would forever change my approach to education and my dedication to preparing students for a world that values the act of helping and mentoring others.

Erin Olson
@eolsonteacher

Following ∨

Honestly, the best assessments I gave were assessments that required someone else to benefit from the students' learning. (gift).
#1to1sbl

6:43 PM - 21 Jan 2015

I'VE SEEN THIS APPROACH PLAY OUT IN SO MANY CLASSES, ACROSS SUBJECTS AND GRADE LEVELS, WITH THE SAME RESULT.

Students are committed to quality work because their audience is important to them.

Students push the boundaries of creativity to show their greatness to others.

Students feel empowered when someone can take their work and do something with it.

What Can They Publish?

Whether it's research, their personal journey and growth in learning, or how their passion might connect to a classroom theme, there is a place for them to publish and teach others. History, science, English, or even math have the potential for student publishing and facilitating learning to transform their classroom.

How Can They Publish?

There are some incredible apps that are perfect for students to create content. Many of them, like Adobe Spark, Book Creator, or Apple's iWork, are all tried and true platforms of creative process. I cannot imagine any of these apps going away in the next five years. The reason for that is that their output methods are focused on creativity. Audio, video, photos, and text are all part and parcel to the creative ecosystem of these apps, and these mediums carry the same weight across all technology and all industries.

When Something Doesn't Exist, Make It Yourself

In the fall, I will be launching a unique and exciting project with one of my high school students, Ariel Mansano, Class of 2020. The project is a podcast called Beyond the Test. The podcast's mission is to connect with professionals who are innovating in their industry and share their

BEYOND THE TEST PODCAST

SCAN QR CODE
WITH YOUR
CAMERA TO LISTEN
TO THE EPISODE.

NEW EPISODE
EVERY THURSDAY!

stories of passion, self-awareness, and pursuit of their dreams with high school students to empower them to believe they could do the same.

You might wonder if this podcast is any different from every other podcast. Before I answer that, let me share some backstory around the project. First, I have a confession to make. I am slightly (not slightly) addicted to podcasts. Whether it's *The GaryVee Audio Experience, CoolCatTeacher, Beyond Influential, Presentable, Cult of Pedagogy,* or *Ditch That Textbook,* I find myself binging on podcasts multiple times a day. I also talk a lot about podcasts with my students in my Entrepreneur Spark Studio course, to the point that it might have started to get annoying. You have *that* question? Have you listened to that podcast? You want to learn about that? There is this one Gary Vee episode. It got to the point that, one day, my student Ariel lodged a complaint against me. He said, "If I want to get into business, there is a podcast. If I want to get into marketing, there is a podcast, but what if I don't know what I want to be? There is no podcast for high school students trying to figure out life!" My knee jerk response was to say, "Well why don't you make your own?" At that point, I realized that creativity and entre-preneurship are more about fixing a problem that others might not notice than anything else. The risky part is being able to identify if the reason no one noticed the problem is because it isn't actually a problem, but that it is another blog post altogether.

So we set out to create that podcast, and this is how we're doing it.

We started with a list of interesting people and industries. We reached out to over thirty people, and much to my chagrin, they actually responded! I say chagrin because this isn't the first time I have launched a podcast, but most people didn't make time for my invitation to be interviewed the first time around. When I said it was with a high school co-host for high school students, the response was swift and welcoming. Interesting, right?

Then we authored a series of foundational questions for two reasons. The first is that by having those "essential questions" with different answers from each guest, we were creating the possibility for incredible anecdotal research around creative problem solving. After recording the first season of ten to fifteen episodes and listening to them while taking notes, we actually have the ability to synthesize the ideas of huge thought leaders, influencers, and recognized professionals in their industries. This still allowed for organic questions, based on the flow of the conversation, to make each episode unique and interesting.

The next step was to set, strategize, and organize communication, scheduling, and the tech end of the project, which in and of itself was a huge challenge to overcome. We traversed FOUR different platforms, as we strove to find the simplest and most reliable ways to record a podcast with someone across the country or the world.

The final piece was to have fun! My co-host shared in an interview, during my ISTE Keynote, that when he was interviewing a former VP at Apple, he was smiling ear to ear the entire time. This is because he had an idea, made a plan, did something about it, and most importantly, was trying to provide value for others.

With guests from Twitch, Snapchat, the Virtual Reality industry, eSports, Social Media Marketing, and a former Apple Exec, this podcast is packed with incredible innovative power.

This podcast is different because it brings value to an audience who is outside of a demographic that most podcasts creators are thinking about.

That is what creativity is all about. Seeing the world differently and doing something about it.

CHAPTER 9

PUT YOUR SOUL INTO IT

The real success is success of the soul.
—Rabbi Joseph Albo

What is a soul? It's like electricity—we don't really know what it is, but it's a force that can light a room.
—Ray Charles

This is where I get a bit Rabbi-ish, but don't be alarmed! The soul is a powerful thing. It's that "extra mile," the "above and beyond," and the "Hey, I didn't know I was capable of that!" all rolled into one. If your brain is the power plant, your soul is the fuel. You can't point to the soul because your soul is you. It's your aura and your essence. An important element of creative success is the personal touch, the unique traits that make you who you are. When you tap into your soul, your ideation can flourish, and you can start to make, solve, and do in a more meaningful way. The reason you can't measure or weigh your soul is because it is boundless. It's capable of creating into infinity—you will never run out of ideas!

The Joy of Unexpected Creativity

When it comes to learning something new, I'm always hungry. If a day or week goes by and I don't learn something new, I feel like telling myself, "Michael, you're doing it wrong." I'm hungry because being a lifelong learner means you're never done, never satisfied, and never complacent. Complacency is poison. The refusal to seek out new ideas, stay abreast of emerging trends, and learn when to pivot and double down on personal and professional growth is toxic. It's toxic for individuals and especially destructive within a large organization, where leaders can succumb to what I call "Blockbuster vision." That's when you see a competitor (Netflix) disrupting your industry with a crazy new way of doing things, but you write them off as a fad and eventually go bankrupt. Complacency keeps you in the same place while the rest of the world moves forward.

In the classroom, the threat of complacency looms large. Educators must fight it daily by stoking their students' hunger for knowledge. If we want kids to master reading, writing, and arithmetic, we have to instill

COMPLACENCY IS POISON

in them a desire to learn and grow. That belief prompted me to launch what I called The Entrepreneurial Spark Studio. At the time, I was about one month into my job as director of innovation at a new school. The new course wasn't designed to teach students how to start their own business. The goal was to make them hungry to learn, discover new things, and maybe cry a little bit too.

After getting started, I was shocked by two things. The first was how many students eagerly volunteered to give up their lunch hour and break periods during the week to take another class. The second was the high level of motivation and dedication I observed in these students while learning on their terms. Think about that. These kids were in school from 7:30 a.m. to 5 p.m. with a nine-period, block schedule, and they *chose* to add a class. Why would they do that? The answer was simple. They loved learning.

I believe everyone loves to learn. Sadly, for many students, desire and joy fade as students are forced into factory-style learning environments. As a result, our schools are lagging a decade behind the real world, leaving many educators skeptical and fearful of emerging or trending technology. The fact that we are still debating technology's role in education in 2018 is proof of the broken system. School systems ban cell phones and social media while their students spend hours outside the classroom hooked to YouTube, Instagram, and Snapchat, doing, guess what? Learning. It might not be your definition of learning, or even mine, but what they're doing fits the textbook definition.

Learning is the process of acquiring and modifying knowledge, behaviors, skills, values, and preferences. Value. In this country, education has decided what is valuable without consulting its primary clients. What other industry does this? Students, I would argue, are the forgotten stakeholders.

How can we captivate the minds of teenagers and expand their creative capacity? By infusing our classrooms with some real-world relevance. Whether it's skills, content, or the ability to acquire knowledge, students must become far more aware of the world around them. Consider the World Economic Forum, a nonprofit think tank founded in 1971. Its massive annual meeting, which commands a global audience and features major world leaders, industry tycoons, artists, musicians, and innovators in a variety of fields, is virtually unknown among most teachers and students. Instead of spending a month reading some antiquated text, our high school students could tune in to the forum and watch thought-provoking discussions on climate change, the arts, education, world trade, and public health. Those real-world conversations could fuel a good portion of the research, analysis, and writing required in the average high school English class. Does that mean dropping *Hamlet* and *To Kill A Mockingbird?* Maybe. If it does, that is yet another symptom of the all-or-nothing mindset infecting our education system.

What's the answer? How can we design a solution to this challenge in an environment refusing to change? How can we boost engagement and motivation while still ensuring that students experience significant growth in understanding and application? It takes an intentionally designed process that isn't student focused but human focused. Design thinking is human focused, and that is what makes solutions sustainable. Here are five tips from my work with The Entrepreneurial Spark Studio to help you expand your students' creative capacity:

1. Survey Students' Interests. (Empathize to understand them.)

Seems basic, but I offered my students the opportunity to tell me about their lives. My survey asked them to rank their interests, and when some students couldn't find their pastime or interest on the list, it was on me to fix that.

2. Help Your Students Become Self-Aware. (Define the problem or challenge.)

Are you self-aware? How did you get there? It was mind-blowing for me, when using a simple, personal development plan, how confused students were when identifying their skills, how those skills might be valuable in a job, their values, or how others perceived their abilities. This plan gave them a roadmap on how to start a process of growth for themselves.

3. Scale Toward Mastery. (Ideate the plan or possibility.)

Students live in moments. Chapters, units, semesters, and school years. When I challenged my students to create an action plan to gain mastery of a skill, for most of them, it was like riding a bike for the first time. When students found that most skills, like app development, product design, and business management, took twenty weeks, six months, two years, or more, they couldn't wrap their heads around how they would achieve this in a semester. The answer was they wouldn't, but that shouldn't stop them. I encouraged them to scale the full scope of the task and do the work. And at the end, they were able to see what twelve to sixteen weeks of growth looked like, reflect on what worked and what didn't, and correct the course. Sort of like life, right?

4. Kick Perfection to the Curb and Start Doing. (Prototype the potential you want to see.)

Prototypes are not clean. They're rough, flawed, and contain errors. They're meant to learn from, to build from, and to ensure that 2.0 is better in every way than 1.0. This concept, borrowed from computational design, is all about learning from use and experience. We don't need to perfect things on the first attempt because most first attempts are flawed. This approach is at odds with traditional education, and we need to fix that. For most students, testing methods to launch their company, learning a new set of skills, or teaming up with others to leverage their unique gifts are completely foreign experiences. I found students asking me questions like, "What if I get halfway through the semester and realize that this isn't the right direction?" or "What happens if I realize that I can't master this skill or launch my product?" My response was always, "Stop. Reflect. Pivot." It was a little confusing, but it made sense. Stop. Reflect. Pivot. I made sure they realized that it's okay to change course and that the new skills you learn on one path can be beneficial when you head in a different direction. When we reject the silo mindset and start showing students how to step into new experiences, they will see how life is much more connected than we realize.

5. Try. You Don't Know Until You Do. (Test toward clarity.)

Traditional schooling does not put much emphasis on applied knowledge. I hate to say it, but memorizing facts and snippets of information might pique interest, but it doesn't lead to any sort of *doing*. No, a diorama doesn't count, and neither does a group project that regurgitates some curricular topic that is a near replica to the other class groups. Students need to experience making something that others use and interact with. As students begin to build prototypes of apps using Google Slides (Stay tuned for that project workflow.), they understand that vision, ideas, and content mean nothing if the experience isn't interesting, clear, and exciting. Creating a service is the same, and testing means not just accepting criticism but actually seeking it out and looking to leverage the criticism to improve whatever it is that you're doing.

This is how I scaled my Entrepreneur Studio courses. This is how I helped students grow. This is how I leveraged the love of learning to get students to grow and develop skills and abilities in ways previously unimaginable. What's even more mind blowing is the level to which they incorporated fundamental literacies and core curricular concepts into their work. Here is the breakdown:

Math—Product Design, App Develop, and Machine Learning—all required advanced problem solving abilities, the understanding of variables, and a significant attention to accuracy.

English—Elevator pitches, presentations, white papers, and research and development all required writing and communication to be accurate, original, and of the highest quality. If you think English teachers are unforgiving, you have never met a venture capitalist.

History—"If you don't understand the past, you are doomed to repeat it" is not just a tagline; it's reality. The ability to research and connect common threads of events and growth in an industry is Business 101.

Science—You want to see chemistry, physics, technology, and product design collide? Build a hoverboard. No joke. When it comes to biotech and other science technology mashups, there are so many ways to take science beyond the STEM scripted experiences.

There are so many ways to take these core literacies and course subjects into the realm of real and relevant. What are you doing to design a recipe for disruption?

WHAT ARE YOU DOING TO DESIGN A RECIPE FOR DISRUPTION?

The Power of Discovery

As I sit with an eleventh-grade student, he starts to share with me how he wants to figure out how Artificial Intelligence (AI) could help people fully control their dreams. It's a mind-blowing idea, but where do you start? He has no clue, and as I try to keep up the persona that educators, or any "experts," know everything, I start asking him questions. Not questions he needs to answer, but rather questions he needs to act on. A big challenge in life is not knowing what you don't know. So what do you do when you don't know something? Not just young people but adults too underestimate the power of the internet to find answers they need or even ones they didn't know they needed. The number one response to nearly eighty percent of questions in my courses is "Google it." Should I know everything, or should I know where to find anything? Digital and internet literacy is as fundamental as writing and reading. So where do you start? How do you become a Google search ninja?

Today, there is absolutely nothing standing in the way of your finding the knowledge you need. You just need to know how to navigate the journey.

In the case of this student, I asked him if his idea was research-focused, manufacture-focused, or service-focused. He said research, so I asked him if he had ever heard of Google Scholar? While some might use that resource as a method to find scholarly articles for college courses, I find it a great way to find experts in research-oriented fields. I broke it down for him as follows:

Step 1: Go to scholar.google.com and search for a topic.

Step 2: Adjust date filter to desired year to include current research.

Step 3: Evaluate if you want to connect with a local expert or a more renowned expert. (Sometimes you're lucky and you get both.)

Step 4: Check the frequency of the work being cited.

Step 5: Google researcher to find contact info, e.g.: faculty website or professional blog.

Step 6: Draft an email explaining how you found them, a line about who you are, and why you're reaching out. Ask them if they would be open to engaging you in a conversation around this topic you are both passionate about.

WHAT DO YOU DO WHEN YOU DON'T KNOW SOMETHING?

It's activities like the one above that can demonstrate to students how research, when used in an actionable way, leads to a better understanding and execution of the discovery process. Research can and should be more than just finding information and regurgitating it back to a teacher in the form of a five-paragraph essay. The above challenge is meant to complement other methods of research. The power in the activity is that it gives students a twofold level of skill, developed both in finding information and discovering how you can use the internet to connect with experts, learn from them, and use them as an information source. It's real world experiences like this that show students how they can engage in a globally connected society through the internet to learn new skills, gain new insights, and engage in collaborative experiences.

Why Teaching Students That Kindness Can Be a Currency Gives Them an Empowering Sense of Purpose

I was invited by a longtime friend to speak to a group of about fifty students who had spent the day engaging in lectures and workshops, focused on business and money through the lens of Torah, aka the Bible. As I stood before them, ready to share my insights and experiences into why kindness might be the greatest business asset and tool for the next decade, a flash of inspiration hit me like a ton of bricks. How *fortunate* these students are to be growing up in 2018, when there is literally *nothing* stopping them from turning their passion into purpose and leveraging technology and collaboration to make it happen. What seemed like a few minutes was only a second or two as I wondered—what if I had sat here as a fifteen-year-old, listening to my own talk about the importance of purpose and self-awareness, emphasizing how important it is to provide value to others? Would I have been able to realize that my current work was my mission? Would I have been able to leverage, dogpile, and AIM to make an impact in a pre-Google/YouTube/Facebook/ etc. world? That's when it finally clicked for me. The tools, mediums, and methods mean nothing if you don't have that purpose and mission-driven inspiration that give you the empowering feeling of resilience to push through and succeed in the face of any challenge. That *sweet spot,* so to speak, is what students are missing out on because, in school, we are taught to define our strengths by how employable they are and how well paid we can be.

When you look at the Ikigai-inspired illustration, nearly every student pointed out that our love of what we do and how much the world needs it are neither emphasized nor discussed. This was even more evident at the end of the forty-five-minute workshop when only one out of fifty of these high schoolers acknowledged he or she had ever engaged in such an experience.

That is why I created the **Kindness Is Currency** Design Driven Experience. This flexible learning experience can span forty minutes to two hours and propel your students into days or weeks of unimaginable and inspiring moments, rooted in sound development of foundational literacies.

KINDNESS IS CURRENCY EBOOK

You can get the Kindness Is Currency eBook at https://thetechrabbi.com/ebdthebook

Why don't students engage in critical thinking that focuses on social good? Why is it that schools cannot find time in the day to help students explore their passion and purpose? Why does it take some extracurricular event to have students say to me, "I have never been challenged to think this way," or "why doesn't school teach us to create solutions to the problems our communities face?" What if that process of discovery would actually motivate them to invest in their English, biology, or world languages classes? Instead, our students' motivation is driven extrinsically by the fear of failing school, thereby failing life. Think about that for a moment when you hear about students having test anxiety to the point that they make themselves ill. The idea that my entire life is dependent upon the success of my first seventeen years of schooling is sad. Are those critical years? Yes. That's exactly what our youth believe, and it is that external pressure that has standardized success and purged our students of nearly all their curiosity and creativity.

Without purpose, there is little to no change of intrinsic motivation, and I leverage my own education journey to fuel my work in fixing this brokenness in education. I graduated high school with less than a 2.0 GPA. Why? The lack of meaning and purpose was doubled with teachers who were not or could not challenge me.

Support Their Passion

For many students, school is one of the few or only places where they can feel safe, supported, and validated in sharing their ideas.

That is why 20-percent time is so important in schools. Giving students 20 percent of their time in school to pursue passions can have a significantly positive impact on their social-emotional well-being. If done right, you can incorporate so many learning opportunities connected to curriculum and skills into those passion-driven projects. When students see that reading, writing, and strong verbal communication skills are needed for them to develop and build up skills around a passion, they see learning with a purpose. So how do you bring 20-percent time into your classroom?

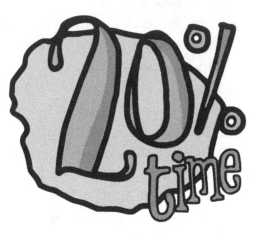

Start with a survey to help students brainstorm and reflect on their interests and enjoyments. Next give the students an action plan to list the skills or resources they need to succeed. After that you set the schedule. Whether it's a Monday morning, Friday afternoon, or Wednesday mid-day, dedicate a specific time to your 20-percent goal and give the students space to create. It will be hard and sometimes foreign for students who are used to being told what to do, how to think, and what to remember. When you give students this space, they will overcome these mental blocks. Once free to explore, they will not disappoint you.

CHAPTER 10

STAY HUMBLE

"We do not see things as they are.
We see things as we are."
—Talmud Brachot 55b

"When we strive to become better than we are,
everything around us becomes better too."
—Paul Coelho

Humility is one of the most important character traits one can acquire. This is because humility leads to joy, and joy can lead to a stronger sense of creativity. Humility isn't a low view of your own importance. Humility isn't self-doubt, low self-esteem, or self-hate. Humility gives us a chance to work hard and do great things while keeping in mind that others' successes do not adversely affect us. It's choosing not to be part of the apple-versus-orange experience, where we think because fruit is fruit, it's the same. Humility gives us the chance to appreciate and enjoy what we have as well as the goodness of others and their work.

What Good Is Humility?

Without humility nothing from this book will provide you with long-term success. Yet the skills, abilities, and success are what allow one to be humble. You see, humility can only come through greatness. This greatness is something that every person has deep inside themselves. It's only revealed through the confidence, persistence, and perseverance that come with hard work. The process of intentional design is most certainly a journey, but its true success and your true success rely on two crucial ingredients. Those are the elements of humility and gratitude.

Humility and honesty create legacy.

Humility is understood to be a modest or low view of one's own importance. So what good is humility? Are we supposed to look at ourselves as worthless or less-than? How is that for a confidence builder? Perseverance, resilience, and all the strengths of triumph cannot be achieved if you feel that you are nothing. A famous scene from the Bible not only changed my view of humility forever but also gave me powerful insight into how humility can be a driver for great work to be achieved and gratefulness to always be at the forefront of one's mind.

The story is of Moses, whom the Bible defines as the humblest of all men. How could the man who split the Red Sea, who grew up among a prophetic mother, father, sister, and brother look at himself as lowly or worthless? Instead the story reveals that Moses had a revolutionary view of the world. He acknowledged his greatness and took the role of a true leader; he believed that his talents were not his own but bestowed upon him, and if anyone had been given the same qualities, they would have done even more with them! This reveals that humility is not a state of being; it's an attitude that allows you to do great work without any obstacles from self-doubt, self-criticism, or others who would obstruct you from reaching your goals with resounding success!

So…

One of the Biggest Obstacles to Creativity Is a Lack of Humility

There is no simple lesson to teach humility. Neither is there some magical moment when you start being humble. The irony of humility is if you have it, you have it; if you say you have it, you've lost it, even if just for a moment. Think of humility as a verb. It is an active state of being that is not a static moment or a stagnant existence. It is found in hard work and perseverance. So how do we model humility and teach it to others? Leading by example is key. Humility means you acknowledge what you have and also what you do. It is being able to admit when you're wrong, or you don't know. Humility is being open to listening to others and being proud to share your own thoughts on the topic at hand. What makes humility the linchpin of innovation is it grounds us with good character traits and the importance of others. Many incredible minds have prioritized innovation at the expense of other people, the planet, and even themselves. Humility keeps us grounded and allows for greatness that brings true value and benefit to the world around us to occur. So how do you develop humility and inculcate it in others around you? These are seven tips:

1. Believe in something bigger than yourself.

Believing in something bigger than yourself keeps you grounded. Without answering to something greater than yourself, you leave room for intellect, reason, and context to guide you into the darkness. For me it's G-d. Surprise! Whether it's G-d for you or not, there needs to be something bigger than you, and we have to teach young people to find that. If you lack it, then there is nothing standing in your way to reach your goal and something that is damaging beyond repair. There are many innovators who sacrificed everything to reach their own personal moonshot. I can't say it is wrong, but it is definitely something that needs to be discussed openly.

2. Be thankful for those around you.

You can't get there alone. I don't care where it is. You must—we must—be thankful for those around us. It is this value that allows us to be leaders who empower and celebrate the success of others. I find this way of thinking to drive some interesting motivation in my life in that I am thankful for my "competition." I am thankful for those in my niche area of work who are doing great things. I learn from them, and they make me a better person.

3. Celebrate others' success.

This leads me to be able to celebrate the success of others. By inculcating in our youth the idea of celebrating others' success, we remove a very aggressive and negative level of competition that begins in our youth and never truly ends. To be able to celebrate the wins of others, we allow for the possibility of being much happier and learning from those people around us. It also leads back to that something that is bigger than you. I can look at a dozen innovators around me and believe that my success, my income, my breakthroughs are not diminished by their achievements, and the same goes for my own.

4. Be wise, not in your own estimation.

"Do not be wise in your own eyes." A strong statement from Proverbs 3:7. So how do you balance your awareness and acknowledgment of your gifts and abilities? Is it even possible to entirely remove one's ego? If you're focused on doing good work and being good to people, your successes will be acknowledged by others. Of course you want to ensure you distance yourself from depression and self-criticism (It is encouraged to celebrate your wins!) and keep a healthy balance of awareness.

5. Forgive quickly.

This one is huge. Forgiveness. Imagine if Edison and Tesla worked as a team. Where would the world be? When we engage in conflict, it is important to forgive quickly. That doesn't mean to be a fool or allow toxic behavior to be tolerated. What it does mean is looking at the big picture of life, moving on from petty disagreements, and forgiving the faults of others. With this approach, innovation has an amazing chance to flourish in your classroom or community.

6. Be a lifelong learner.

A true testament to your level of humility is your level of teachability. Can you be taught? Think about that for a moment. We expect it of our students, right? Being teachable means learning from everyone, including your students, novice colleagues, and even the forty-year, veteran teacher. Everyone has a voice, and everyone has something of value to be shared. I cannot stress this enough. A lack of teachability is like a forty-foot, brick wall between a person and potential innovation. Bottom line—be teachable.

7. You *enjoy* helping others.

I am guilty of this to the extreme. The whole reason I left the design and marketing industry was due to my absolute love for helping others. The feeling of satisfaction and sheer joy I experience when someone masters a skill I mentored them in is huge for me. It is the reason that I got into teaching and made my way back into the classroom, even after a few years of traveling the world consulting. Wherever it is, innovation thrives in a space where your passion to help others is the main focus of your work.

Feeling a little more humble? It is a lifelong journey but something that can be powerfully internalized, if emphasized and refined throughout the early years of a student's education. The more humble we are, the more open we are to change, the more teachable we become. The more teachable we become, the more we will enjoy helping others and celebrating their success. The end game? A better world for sure.

Cultivating Humility

Teaching humility is done through modeling it, building up students, encouraging them to be the best they can be, and most importantly, never embarrassing them. If students learn early on to be grateful for their skills and success, then they are much more likely to be humble, kind, and caring, regardless of how successful they become. Remind them that humility doesn't mean we are perfect or devoid of mistakes and failures. Humility means that regardless of what happens, we have an appreciation, a viewpoint rooted in kindness, and a life mission statement of bringing value to the world around us. It is only with that kind of humility and honest reflection and respect that we can leave a legacy in the hearts and minds of those we serve. And that's how we will change the world—one person at a time.

Be passionate. Put your soul into it. And stay humble. Always.

CHAPTER 11

CULTIVATING CREATIVITY TOOLKIT

WWW.THETECHRABBI.COM/STORE

Perfection—or the desire for it—too often prevents us from testing our creativity. We tend to avoid putting ourselves in positions where we might appear to be struggling, failing, or simply "not getting it." This is the roadblock to creative thinking. To bolster a more creative you, experiences that lead to struggle, failure, and things not making sense are prerequisites. Those kinds of challenges are what make a person a lifelong learner versus a seasoned veteran. If we wait until we know everything, we never will accomplish anything. Creativity isn't some abstract eureka moment. Creativity is taking two good ideas and mashing them up into great ones. It's practical, usable, and beneficial for others. Creativity is about thinking, making, and doing, and the time to start is now.

Throughout this book, there have been activities and challenges that complement each chapter's step to building creative courage and capacity. The ideas and experiences below are more recipes to cook up some creative awesomeness. Whether you engage in them on your own or collaborate with others, you will find that there is greatness hidden in the journey, waiting to be revealed in all of us.

The Torrance Test of Creative Thinking (TTCT)

This creativity test defines divergent thinking in four ways:

- **Fluency**—how many uses you can come up with
- **Originality**—how uncommon those uses are (e.g., "router restarter" is more uncommon than "holding papers together")
- **Flexibility**—how many areas your answers cover (e.g., cufflinks and earrings are both accessories, aka one area)
- **Elaboration**—level of detail in responses; "keeping headphones from getting tangled up" would be worth more than "bookmark"

The test is an incredible window into our current creative capacity, so we can work toward building a stronger creative thought process within ourselves. The following link takes you to a scaled down version of the test. The results will help you understand eight different metrics of your current creative abilities: **testmycreativity.com**

30 Circle Activity

Disclaimer: If you are not familiar with the 30 Circle Challenge, then you must go through the activity before reading it. The challenge is eye-opening to our self-imposed obstacles to creative thinking and is a great way to learn more about how you creatively solve problems. Consider scanning the QR code below and going through the activity before reading further.

This activity is about promoting divergent thinking. I have shared, many times, that developing a creative mindset is very similar to running a marathon. Sure, you can wake up the morning of and start running but don't expect that to be your best possible plan to success. I have run this activity dozens of time and seen so many struggle with this activity, including me! When I ask my students or teachers how many drew a baseball, a majority of hands usually go up. Then I ask them how many drew a basketball or a golf ball, and what we find as a group is that we identify a solution and then create micro advancements to ensure we succeed within the constraints of time. Whether it's balls, emoji faces, planets, or clocks, this exercise gives us a very powerful window into our own creative capacity.

Spoiler alert!!!

Read the directions—in three minutes, turn as many circles as you can into recognizable objects. No thinking about this for a minute. Where does it say "each circle" or anything indicating that you cannot simply draw a square around the page and say, "Polka dot blanket, mic drop, done?"

Created by Bob McKim, Head of Design School at Stanford

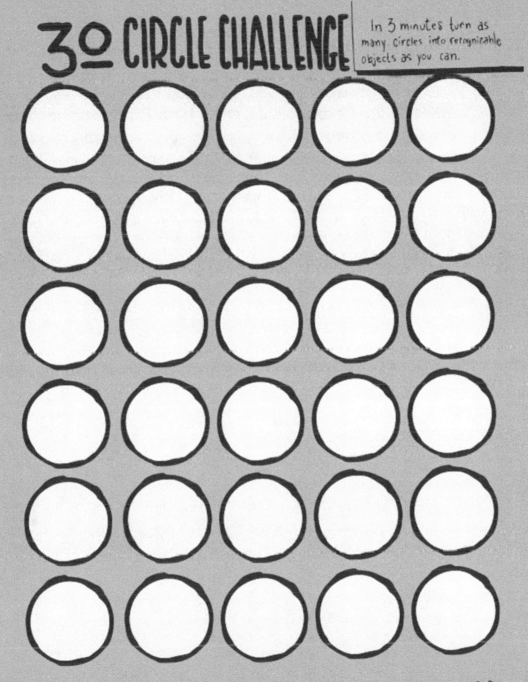

Alternative Uses

Developed by J.P. Guilford in 1967, the Alternative Uses Test stretches your creativity by giving you two minutes to think of as many uses as possible for an everyday object like a chair, coffee mug, or brick. This practice in divergent thinking allows you to strengthen your ability to find correlations between ideas, objects, and activities. The test traditionally uses a brick, chair, or paperclip as an example, but you're free to come up with your own. While some of us struggle beyond ten alternative uses, younger students tend to find upwards to fifty or more.

Combo Photo Project

During many talks, I share that **creativity is a mindset, not an art set.** The elephant in the room is once you buy into the mantra, what steps can you take to act on the mindset? There are so many cool ways to build up our creative abilities. What I am striving to do with all my work on the *Educated By Design* project is to discover ways in which creative exercises can complement development of fundamental literacies and competencies to make our students and ourselves more capable of doing great work.

For those who have yet to see the work from Stephen McMennamy, you are in for a treat. His ability to look at the world around him and find creative connections in seemingly divergent objects is uncanny.

CHECK OUT HIS WORK AT INSTAGRAM.COM/COMBOPHOTO

I have followed him on Instagram for close to a year now, and at one point a few months ago, I realized that his creative process could be translated into not just a powerful art project but also an incredible experience in strengthening divergent and creative thinking abilities. With his work as inspiration, I opened up Adobe Photoshop but soon realized that this needed to be something scalable beyond Photoshop users. So with the famous Geico line in my head, "So Easy a Caveman Can Do It," I set in my mind that it needs to be "So Easy a First Grader Can Do It."

With this line as my inspiration, I opened up Adobe Spark to see how quickly and easily I could create something like Stephen, and here you have it, folks.

My suitcase-Beetle, typewriter-laptop, and gumball-trolly.

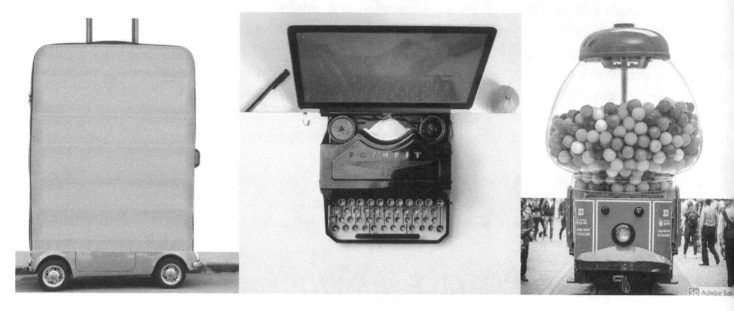

The experience made me realize that to really understand our creative selves and creative potential, we need small concrete moments of eye-opening experiences. We need to dispel the myth that creativity is defined as drawing, painting, or music composition. Most importantly, we need to realize that creativity can be unlocked by looking beyond the functional fixedness of the world and find ways to capture and communicate what we see in new ways.

Combine Photo Challenge

Inspired by Stephen McMennamy

*Teacher Note: You are encouraged to not show project examples. The challenge is meant to not just create but to also drive meaningful discussion and reflective writing. Each element, from creation to discussion to reflection, will help students document their growth around divergent thinking and creativity.

1. Three minutes: Try to write down a list of as many objects as you can.
2. Ten minutes: Brainstorm the features of each object on your list.
    a) Up to you if you share examples, e.g., wheels, cord, rectangle, hole, switch, color, etc.
    b) Choose six objects that you will combine to create three new creations.
3. Thirty minutes: Using Adobe Spark:
    a) Search for two images that represent the chosen objects.
    b) Line them up either vertically or horizontally. The goal is symmetry and to line up the edges of both objects.
    c) Move the border bars and zoom in on each photograph to line up the object as seamlessly as possible.
4. Ten minutes: Share student work with guided discussion around the process and product.
    a) Example Questions:
        i) How did you discover that the two objects connected?
        ii) What was harder—coming up with the list of objects or finding ways to combine them?
        iii) How many different ways did you try to combine the object before deciding on the final combination?
        iv) What did combining "object x" and "object y" tell us about how we look at objects around us?

    v) What are some examples of objects that have been combined that changed the world? (e.g., iPhone, lightbulb, mobile home, Hovercraft)

This activity is something that can be completed in a short amount of time but yields powerful results. Beyond mastery of awesome tech tools like Adobe Spark and the power of imagery and design, this activity gives students an opportunity to create a product that stimulates conversation and awareness around the divergent thinking and creative processes.

It also shows our students and us that creativity is about combining the unexpected, not just drawing it.

Combine + Innovate Challenge

This challenge is one of my favorites. It drives my high school students crazy because it doesn't just require you to think outside of the box; it requires you to use the box. There have been many iterations of this over the years by various designers and professors, but its inception is rooted in a Japanese phenomenon called Chindogu, the Japanese art of inventing gadgets that seem to solve a problem but are, in fact, useless. The challenge pushes you to the limits of divergent thinking and is an incredible way to engage in collaboration. The project timeline is as follows:

- Twenty-four to seventy-two hour activity
- Pick a random object card out of each box (two in total).
- Brainstorm with your team how to combine the two objects to create a new invention or a functional improvement.
- Sketch out or build your prototype.
- Present to the class your product AND process.

Upon completion I have the students showcase their prototypes and give the group a few minutes to walk around and observe others work. They then present their product as well as the process, the latter being the most important part of the challenge. I ask them questions like:

- At what point did you first face challenge?
- How did you start to solve your problem?
- How many ideas did you come up with before the one you are presenting?
- How many variations do you have of this idea?

Many times students will come up with one to three ideas. Then they will go through one iteration with no variation and then turn in their final product.

That might work for worksheets and essays, but it doesn't work for anything that would be defined as innovative in product or practice.

Kindness Is Currency

I strongly believe that creativity thrives in a space where you are striving to help others and providing them value. The *Kindness Is Currency* eBook is a result of my experiences in education where students attempt to bring that vision of creativity into the world. The book is focused on using design thinking to drive experience and requires some background knowledge of Design Thinking for those who do not have experience leading a group along the process. You can watch videos (QR Codes below) before starting with the activities and conversation found in the book. The book challenges students to use the knowledge and skills they have to define community, research challenges and struggles, and ideate a solution that works best for their community. The project can take as long as a few days and expands into weeks and months, depending on your comfort with the process and the freedom and flexibility around content coverage. Students should be encouraged to present their product or plan to their identified community and then spend time reflecting on the experience in its entirety. The eBook contains both an action plan template for your students as well as an innovative practice rubric that hits multiple ELA Common Core standards.

INTRO TO DESIGN THINKING

YOUTUBE PLAYLIST

KINDNESS IS CURRENCY

INTERACTIVE EBOOK

Bad Ideas Factory

Years ago I heard about the "Bad Idea Factory" at a conference. I wish I remembered who presented it or where it occurred, but it was around 2014. Like any buzzword, I tried to plumb the depths of Google to find the creator of these awesome activities. The best I could find was a 2012 article by Kevin Brookhouser titled, *20% Project: Bad Idea Factory*. In the article, he shares that he came up with the term Bad Idea Factory after attending a workshop with Ewen McIntosh at NoTosh. He links to his site, but the link is broken. I reached out to Ewen on Twitter to get more information.

I have used the *Bad Idea Factory* activity many times in various classes ranging from first grade to twelfth. The results are always a blend of entertaining and meaningful experiences because the activity helps everyone involved break down our bias around our own creative abilities and how we evaluate "good ideas."

A great introduction for any class to the activity is a video compilation of *Good Idea, Bad Idea* segments from one of my all-time favorite cartoon shows, *Animaniacs*. The meaning (IMO) of the segments is not just to provide viewers with comedy and entertainment but to also challenge them to actually think. Rare for a cartoon, but *Animaniacs* was ahead of its time.

The Process

The process of the activity is simple and straightforward.

1. Students (or teachers) have X amount of minutes to come up with a list of *as many* "bad ideas" as possible. In the past, I have set a minimum limit around twenty for older students, fifth grade and up. Younger students tend to be excited with the idea that we are challenging them to use their minds and the freedom to show how much they know.

2. Any and all ideas should be documented on whiteboards, posters, or butcher paper, so they can be presented later.

3. Guidelines and good judgment should precede the activity. Encourage students to come up with their own list of guidelines of what "bad ideas" are not appropriate. In the past, my class guidelines have included: No violence, prejudice, or disrespect to any person or people in any way, shape, or form. For older students, you might need to remind them that ideas should be safe and not sexual in nature. Yes, you might get a laugh for a moment, but then we can move on to the activity.

4. Once the ideas are created, students can then analyze their ideas. The following guided questions (Or create your own!) might help spark curiosity and conversation:

   a) How might this "bad idea" be turned into a "good idea"?

   b) Is this idea practical or within your ability to implement?

5. Next is the process of Synthesis. Challenge the students to synthesize their list and find ways that some ideas might combine with others again, using guided questions (or create your own!).

   c) What do each, or some, of your ideas have in common?

   d) How might we borrow something from one idea and add it to another?

6. After this process, they should be able to cut their list down to two or three ideas. After this the students will present their "best bad idea" to the class, which, depending on the class size, could take over an hour. I limit talks to between one to two minutes. No less and no more.

Now what?

Some teachers take this activity to the next level and use it for students to help find a topic for a 20-percent time project. I think the project in and of itself has even greater worth as a way to build creative confidence and courage.

BIBLIOGRAPHY

"Back To School." *LEGO Education*. 2018. Education.lego.com, education.lego.com/en-us/about-us/back-to-school.

Brown, Morgan. "Airbnb: The Growth Story You Didn't Know." *GrowthHackers*. growthhackers.com/growth-studies/airbnb.

Guilford, J. P. *The Nature of Human Intelligence*. New York, New York: McGraw-Hill, 1967. "How Not to Land an Orbital Rocket Booster." YouTube, 2:09. Posted by "SpaceX," 2018, youtu.be/bvim4rsNHkQ.

Hustwit, Gary, and Rams Dieter. *Rams*. Documentary by Film First Co. 2018.

Jobs, Steve. "Stanford Commencement Address." Keynote Address, Stanford University, Stanford, California, June 12, 2005.

Mayer, Richard E. *Multimedia Learning*. New York, NY: Cambridge University Press, 2009.

McBurney, Sally, director. *Steve Jobs: Visionary Entrepreneur*. Silicon Valley Historical Association, 2013.

Mya. "FullTimeKid Channel Trailer." YouTube, 0:35, Posted by "FullTimeKid," 2018, youtube.com/user/FullTimeKid.

Ormrod, Jeanne Ellis. *Educational Psychology: Developing Learners*. Boston, Massachusetts: Pearson/Allyn & Bacon, 2011.

Reingold, Jennifer. "Hondas in Space." *Fast Company*, 1 Feb. 2005, fastcompany.com/52065/hondas-space.

Resnick, Mitchel. "Rethinking learning in the digital age." YouTube, 11:53, Posted by "Serious Science," 2017, youtube.com/watch?v=A_0XzM34_Ew.

Schneersohn, Joseph Isaac, and Menachem Mendel Schneerson. *Hayom Yom: Day By Day*. New York, New York; Kehot, 1988.

Acknowledgments

I want to personally thank the following people. Without you I would have not had the creative courage or capacity to turn "just an idea" into something worth sharing.

My students: Over the past ten years, you have driven me to better myself as an educator and ensure that all students are given a chance to reveal their innate creativity.

Dave and Shelley Burgess: Thank you for believing in my work and investing in turning it into a reality. I am forever grateful for your support.

Erin K. Casey, Mariana Lenox, and the entire My Writers' Connection team: Thank you for helping me shape and refine my work into the book it is today.

To the educators and creativity instigators that mentor me, inspire me, and help me grow:

Jason Ablin, Ai Addyson-Zhang, Brian Aspinall, Tanya Avrith, Math Baier, Susan M. Bearden, Adam Bellow, Ela Ben-Ur, Dani Boepple, Rabbi Yonah Bookstein, Jeff Bradbury, Kristen Brooks, Elyse Burden, Monica Burns, Amy Burvall, Eric Chagala, Ross Cooper, Billy Corcoran, Michelle Cordy, Jon Corippo, George Couros, Alec Couros, Kelly Croy, Dr. Theresa Cullen, Vicki Davis, Kayla Delzer, Steve Dembo, Bob Dillon, Sylvia Duckworth, Leslie Fisher, Laura Fleming, Ben Forta, Yossi Frankel, Camilla Gagliolo, Clara Galán, Don Goble, Sue Gorman, Jenny Grabiec, Jody Green, Dr. Tim Green, Matthew Grundler, Laura Grundler, Yonatan Hambourger, Paul Hamilton, Rebecca Hare, Tony Hawk, Michael Hernandez, Manuel S. Herrera, Bethany Hill, Dr. Beth Holland, Carl Hooker, Cathy Hunt, Felix Jacomino, Lisa Johnson, Maxx Judd, AJ Juliani, Alice Keeler, Zev Kessler, Kurt Klynen, Christine Klynen, Dan Koch, Ann Kozma, Greg Kulowiec,

Rick St. Laurent, Metuka Daisy Lawrence, Mike Lawrence, Rabbi Moshe Levin, Deborah Littman, John Maeda, Ariel Mansano, Katie Martin, Tara Martin, Michael Matera, Shawn McCusker, Scott McLeod, Bryan Miller, Matt Miller, Tom Murray, Sara Murray, Todd Nesloney, Alexis Newman, Erin Olson, Don Orth, Eric Patnoudes, Sam Patterson, Tzvi Pittinsky, Sabba Quidwai, Dr. Kaleb Rashad, Larry Reiff, Mitch Resnick, Reshan Richards, Tisha Richmond, Mike Rohde, Gail Ross-McBride, Dan Ryder, Tina Seelig, Aryeh Siegel, Bill Selak, John Spencer, Rabbi Y. Boruch Sufrin, Rabbi Aryeh Sufrin, Zach Swigard, Sue Thotz, Cate Tolnai, Alberto Valdes, Tony Vincent, Rabbi Avrohom Wagshul, Brad Waid, Inge Wassman, Don Wettrick, Jennifer Williams, Vinney Williams Jr., Elaine Wrenn, Ilana Zadok, Claudio Zavala Jr., Yong Zhao and the many other names I inevitably missed who deserve credit for supporting me on this creative journey.

BRING MICHAEL COHEN TO YOUR SCHOOL OR EVENT

Michael believes that helping people build their creative capacity makes them stronger and more determined problem solvers. Over the past four years, he has traveled the country working with administrators, educators, and students, helping to create programs designed to foster divergent and creative thinking that leverages collaboration, technology, and design thinking to give everyone the tools to solve interesting problems.

Michael shares his story, insights, and ideas with a mix of humor, spiritual insight, hand-drawn slides, and a new vision for education that keeps his audience engaged, entertained, and empowered to be the change they want to see in education.

Michael offers the unique perspective of six years of work in the design and marketing industry, pushing the boundaries of creative process, developing an empathetic perspective for clients, and helping people solve their visual communication challenges before embarking on an over ten-year journey in the field of education. His experiences as a designer, business owner, spiritual mentor, educator, and administrator help him encourage those who work with him to embrace diverse perspectives and always look at how they can be lifelong learners and examples for our youth.

Popular Keynotes and Workshops

1. Educated by Design: Discovering the Potential in the Unconventional
2. Cultivating Problem Solving Skills with Design Thinking
3. 5 Reasons Why Every Student Needs to Think Like a Designer
4. Ignite the Spark in Students Through Visual Design and Communication

Let's Connect

Connect with Michael Cohen for more information about bringing him to your event.
- Email: mcohen@thetechrabbi.com
- Twitter: @TheTechRabbi
- Instagram: @TheTechRabbi
- Blog: educatedbydesign.com
- Youtube: youtube.com/thetechrabbi

DAVE BURGESS Consulting, Inc.

Since 2012, DBCI has been publishing books that inspire and equip educators to be their best. For more information on our DBCI titles or to purchase bulk orders for your school, district, or book study, visit DaveBurgessConsulting.com/DBCBooks.

More from the Like a PIRATE Series™

Teach Like a PIRATE by Dave Burgess
eXPlore Like a Pirate by Michael Matera
Learn Like a Pirate by Paul Solarz
Play Like a Pirate by Quinn Rollins
Run Like a Pirate by Adam Welcome

Lead Like a PIRATE Series

Lead Like a PIRATE by Shelley Burgess and Beth Houf
Balance Like a Pirate by Jessica Cabeen, Jessica Johnson, and Sarah Johnson
Lead with Culture by Jay Billy
Lead with Literacy by Mandy Ellis

Leadership & School Culture

Culturize by Jimmy Casas
Escaping the School Leader's Dunk Tank by Rebecca Coda and Rick Jetter
The Innovator's Mindset by George Couros
Kids Deserve It! by Todd Nesloney and Adam Welcome
Let Them Speak by Rebecca Coda and Rick Jetter
The Limitless School by Abe Hege and Adam Dovico
The Pepper Effect by Sean Gaillard
The Principled Principal by Jeffrey Zoul and Anthony McConnell
The Secret Solution by Todd Whitaker, Sam Miller, and Ryan Donlan
Start Right Now by Todd Whitaker, Jeffrey Zoul, and Jimmy Casas
Stop Right Now by Jimmy Casas and Jeffrey Zoul
Unmapped Potential by Julie Hasson and Missy Lennard
Your School Rocks by Ryan McLane and Eric Lowe

Technology & Tools

50 Things You can Do with Google Classroom by Alice Keeler and Libbi Miller
50 Things to Go Further with Google Classroom by Alice Keeler and Libbi Miller
140 Twitter Tips for Educators by Brad Currie, Billy Krakower, and Scott Rocco
Code Breaker by Brian Aspinall
Google Apps for Littles by Christine Pinto and Alice Keeler
Master the Media by Julie Smith
Shake Up Learning by Kasey Bell
Social LEADia by Jennifer Casa-Todd
Teaching Math with Google Apps by Alice Keeler and Diana Herrington

Teaching Methods & Materials

All 4s and 5s by Andrew Sharos

Ditch That Homework by Matt Miller and Alice Keeler

Ditch That Textbook by Matt Miller

The EduProtocol Field Guide by Marlena Hebern and Jon Corippo

Instant Relevance by Denis Sheeran

LAUNCH by John Spencer and A.J. Juliani

Make Learning MAGICAL by Tisha Richmond

Pure Genius by Don Wettrick

Shift This! by Joy Kirr

Spark Learning by Ramsey Musallam

Sparks in the Dark by Travis Crowder and Todd Nesloney

Table Talk Math by John Stevens

The Classroom Chef by John Stevens and Matt Vaudrey

The Wild Card by Hope and Wade King

The Writing on the Classroom Wall by Steve Wyborney

Inspiration, Professional Growth & Personal Development

4 O'Clock Faculty by Rich Czyz

Be REAL by Tara Martin

Be the One for Kids by Ryan Sheehy

The EduNinja Mindset by Jennifer Burdis

How Much Water Do We Have? by Pete and Kris Nunweiler

P Is for Pirate by Dave and Shelley Burgess

The Path to Serendipity by Allyson Aspey

Sanctuaries by Dan Tricarico

Shattering the Perfect Teacher Myth by Aaron Hogan

Stories from Webb by Todd Nesloney

Talk to Me by Kim Bearden

The Zen Teacher by Dan Tricarico

Children's Books
Dolphins in Trees by Aaron Polansky
The Princes of Serendip by Allyson Apsey

ABOUT THE AUTHOR

Michael Cohen, MSEd, known as The Tech Rabbi, is a designer and technologist turned educator. As a speaker, writer, and creativity instigator, he's on a mission to help young people develop the creative confidence they need to become challenge seekers and solution designers.

He works with schools, institutions, and businesses to help them create or refine opportunities for students to leverage technology, media creation, and digital age skills in ways that foster inquiry and the drive to solve the complex challenges of our global society.

Cohen shares his story of design and creativity through social media, keynote addresses, and featured talks on international stages, including ISTE, SXSW EDU, Congreso .Edu Mexico, EdTechTeacher Summits, and Apple Education events.

He currently serves as the director of innovation at Yeshiva University of Los Angeles Boys School (YULA), where he's focused on scaling a student-driven entrepreneurial studio. He's an Apple Distinguished Educator, Google Certified Trainer, and Adobe Certified Trainer and has been ranked as one of today's top fifty edtech influencers.

He lives in Los Angeles, California, with his wife and four children and loves to rock climb, skateboard, and build forts.

CPSIA information can be obtained
at www.ICGtesting.com
Printed in the USA
LVHW102224290319
612402LV00005B/10/P

9 781949 595109